In and Out of
Our Own Way

In and Out of Our Own Way

The teaching stories of
Bennet Wong & Jock McKeen

© 1995 B. Wong and J. McKeen. All rights reserved

PD Publishing
Haven By-the-Sea
RR#1, 240 Davis Road
Gabriola Island, British Columbia, Canada V0R 1X0

Canadian Cataloguing in Publication Data

Wong, Bennet, 1930–
In and out of our own way

Includes bibliographical references
ISBN 0-9696755-2-6

1. Wong, Bennet, 1930– —Anecdotes. 2. McKeen, Jock,
1946– —Anecdotes. 3. Self-actualization (Psychology)
4. Interpersonal relations. I. McKeen, Jock, 1946– II. Title.
BF637.S4W65 1995   158   C95-911071-2

Published under the auspices of the *Journal of Child and Youth Care.*

Printed and bound in Canada

∞ This book is printed on acid-free paper.

Dedication

Dedicated to our parents and our sons,
who are an integral part of our stories.

Contents

Introduction ix

Island 1

Toilet Training 2

Breath Holding 3

Supersalesman 4

Singing Softly 5

Arguments with Mother 6

Musician 6

Liver 8

Chink 9

Prejudice 11

Family Secret 13

A Boy's Secret 14

On the Bridge 15

Self-esteem 19

Remembering Who I Am 20

Fraternity 22

Buying Real Estate 23

Lessons in Finance 24

Junior Red Cross Life Saving Badge 28

Serendipity 29

Tennis Champion 30

My Father 32

Yogic Bliss 34

God Is Good 36

Physical Labour 37

Making Work Meaningful 38

Brief Therapy 40

Tricked Into Awareness 42

Keeping Up with Crime 44

Cowardice 46

Cool Head 49

Learning How to Receive 52

Forgiveness 54

Loving Is My Pleasure 56

Self-delusion 57

Reality Check 59

First Impression 60

Dignity 62

Star-struck 64

Aikido 65

Look Before You Leap! 66

Tai Ji Master 67

Cowboy 70

Honesty 73

Cocktail Parties 74

A Public Display 76

The End of Innocence 77

Inclusion 79

Unrequited Love 80

Overcoming Repulsions 82

Pain Phobia 83

My First Encounter with Death 85

Phillip 86

Fatigue 88

My Day in Heaven 90

Sparkles 92

The Pain of Compassion 94

Standing Firm 95

A Fear of Zen Flying 97

Fear of Flying 99

Letting Go 101

The Fourth Dimension 102

Possession 104

Capitulation.. 106

Explaining the Inexplicable 107

Hero 109

Skiing 111

A Cure for Height Phobia 113

Vulnerability 116

Genes and Memes 117

Father-Son Talks 119

Teaching Autonomy 120

Little Emperors 122

Meaning What You Say... 124

Whining 125

Through Parents' Eyes 127

A "Sensitive" Child 128

Straight and Tall.. 130

A Scottish Solution 131

Non-presence 134

Presence 136

Learning Non-presence 138

Never Get Discouraged 140

Intimacy 141

Rejection 143

Jealousy... 144

Avoiding Abandonment 146

From Romance to Power Struggle 147

Flow.. 149

The Landscape of Our Lives 151

The Pit 152

Reps' Stories... 154

References 157

Introduction

I have always enjoyed Ben's stories about himself. In workshops, and in leisure times, he talks about his life and his experiences in a way that others find both entertaining and insightful. He is always ready to laugh at himself, and to show his imperfections, and to describe his struggles in coming to terms with the challenges of his life. In workshops, when he tells his stories, I watch as so many people are moved by the simple, yet profound, messages that come through his talks. I notice that people can identify with him, since he is so open to share his insecurities, and his personal confrontations.

The stories he tells about me have been a different matter; I have had to learn to enjoy them. At the beginning, I was quite uncomfortable with his humorous, yet caring, accounts of my gaffes and personal struggles. To cover my insecurities, I have tended to put on a front of perfection that makes me difficult to know. As Ben would recount yet another story about me, in which I was the fall guy, I noticed that people came to know me better by his telling, and warmed up to me, and could identify with me. And I learned that his gibes and jokes were indications of his caring and of his intimate knowledge about the depth of me. Underneath my set exterior, the mess of my life is something that people can relate to, if they can see it. So, now that I have recognized that there is much to be gained by such open and humorous accounts, I have tried to tell more stories about myself, and my friendship with Ben.

I wanted Ben to set down his stories into a book, so that people could read and re-read them. At my repeated prompting, he has gathered together the collection that appears in this book. I had originally intended that this book would include his stories only, for people to enjoy. As his writing progressed, he found that many of his stories involved events that he and I had shared together. So, he invited me to include some of my accounts of events as I experienced them. Rather shyly, I am including some offerings from myself here too. His request for me to include some stories has been challenging to me; I feel somewhat diffident in face of his vignettes that offer such warmth and self-acceptance and humour. To make for clear reading, the stories written by me will be enclosed in a box; Ben's stories will appear unboxed on the pages.

We both hope you find something for yourself in these pages. We laughed and cried and struggled when we experienced these stories initially; hopefully you will find your own feelings, and will recall some of your own learning tales.

Jock McKeen

 Our relationship is a tapestry of lived stories, some colorful, some sombre, some light, some dark. At various times, they are woven together in a loose, relaxed fashion; at other times, they are tightened into knots that hurt. No matter, from them all we have learned so much about ourselves and one another.

. . . Bennet Wong

Island

Early adolescence was a difficult period for me. Being Chinese, I knew that I was different from the other kids. I was terrible at sports; physically, I was skinny and weak; because of our family's economic situation, I could not afford to dress in style, even if I knew what that meant. It was evident to me that I was clearly excluded from the social life that was burgeoning at high school. Although my classmates seemed to like me in everyday interaction, I received no invitations to the parties and social events that the "in crowd" was enjoying. I had few friends. I felt alone and isolated on an island that was no choice of my own.

At that time, I stumbled across John Donne's lines from his *Meditations*: "No man is an island unto himself." Although all of my life's experience seemed to be opposite to that, those lines gave me hope. Peering from the shores of my isolated island, across the waters of all the social interactions that separated me from all of the other islands, I could see that people were actively visiting one another's islands—but not mine!

Determined to become an appealingly visitable island, I set about the task of beautifying my shores. I moved things around, hid the unattractive things, trotted out what I believed would win acceptance. On my island, the swamps and marshes were drained, rocks moved, lawns seeded and flowers planted. I cut my hair in style and bought some new clothes and sat on my shores, waiting for the visiting boats that would surely take note. I sat and dispiritedly watched the active social scene of boats busily plying back and forth between the other islands. None came to mine.

Now resigned to my fate of social isolation, I decided to devote my attention to exploration of my own shores. I returned all of my things—the rocks, the swamps, the marshes—back to their natural state. I dug deep beneath my surface, discovering things about myself that I could appreciate and value—precious stones and useful natural resources. These I could mine and process for my own pleasure, even if they would never be appreciated by the other islands. That task became my spiritual search and shaped my destiny.

While rummaging in the depths of myself, I suddenly stumbled upon another person devoted to a similar task with himself. We met, we touched, and we were both amazed! I had the sudden recognition that the waters of social interaction that divided our islands are only *surface illusions*! Beneath those illusions, our shores are continuous with one another. Indeed, at our deepest levels, at the core, we all are one and the same! That revelation changed my life forever.

Now I know that I am never alone.

Toilet Training

In my work with people, I have always had difficulty with trying to ascertain the accuracy of recalled memories, especially those of childhood. In my own life, the event of my toilet training stands out for me—an event that I discovered could be corroborated by my sisters who were present. In my large family, older siblings did much of the parenting, so much of my toilet training was in their hands.

I remember sitting on a pot, having just successfully completed the task of defecation. I see the hands of my sisters placing sheets of paper in front of me, encouraging me to take them and wipe myself. I can feel the rising stubbornness in my lower lip and chest as I refuse to listen to their pleas. "Why won't you even try?" they implore. To this day, I remember my determined refusal. "I know you guys—if I do it once, I'll have to *always* do it!" To my sorrow, I learned that I was right!

Breath Holding

As a little boy, I was very controlling indeed. I discovered that I could use a myriad of approaches to control the adults around me. When my parents would leave me with my grandmother, I would lie at the door, sniffing the crack to inhale the remnants of the air they had just vacated. I would pout loudly when I did not get my own way. And when all else failed, I would hold my breath.

One day, my parents and I were at a variety store, and they refused to buy me some candy that I wanted. And so, I set out to show them. I held my breath all the way through the check-out counter, and continued as we walked down the street. We got some distance when I collapsed on the grass from hypoxia. My mother had the presence of mind to cry out to my amused father, "Oh no! He's dead. We'll have to get a shovel and bury him." At which point, I jumped up and let them know that I was not dead, and that such drastic measures were not called for. But I still tried to get them with the old breath-holding move. In order to outplay me, they took to carrying a shovel in the trunk of the car. Whenever I would hold my breath, they would say, "Get the shovel! He's gone for sure now."

Jock

Often, your mind is adult,
while your body is four years old.

. . . Bennet Wong

Supersalesman

I was raised in a large Chinese Canadian family that worked hard to survive, first running a small restaurant in a rural Saskatchewan town, then a grocery store. All of us children began to work as soon as we were physically capable. When I was 12 years old, I was already priding myself on being a competent young grocery clerk, able to provide information, handle money and above all, to *keep our customers happy!* It was during the World War II years when everything was rationed; our policy was to mete out scarce commodities such as paper products and canned goods to our "regular" customers.

On one busy day in the store when we were crowded with customers, I was serving a matronly, haughty woman whom I was determined to impress. She quietly asked me for a box of Kotex, which was one of the paper products that was in short supply. Unfortunately, I had never received any sex education; left to my own imagination, I had assumed that Kotex was only another brand of tissues similar to Kleenex. Although Kleenex was also scarce, we had just received a supply, which I was proud to be able to offer her.

In front of waiting customers, in a large, authoritative adolescent voice I declared, "I'm sorry that we have no Kotex, but we *do* have Kleenex *which is just as good!*" Suddenly, the chattering of the customers ceased and the store fell silent as all eyes turned in my direction. I had obviously committed some heinous act, the nature of which entirely escaped my understanding. To make matters worse, my father swooped in from what was now alien space, dragging me by the scruff of my neck into the dark recesses of the back of the store. I was told to stay there and not speak to anyone.

I remained ignorant as to the nature of my crime for many following years. One day in my later adolescence, I read about the nature and mechanism of menstruation, and I was flooded with a sense of humiliation. Worse still, I was embarrassed for that unfortunate woman whose biological functions I had so publicly exposed because of my ignorant pride in being such a good salesman!

Singing Softly

All of my life, I have loved the human voice and music; my admiration of singers has been boundless. When I was 14 years old, I joined the junior choir of a local church, enjoying the opportunity to belong to a group of peers who could sing so beautifully. Choir practice became the highlight of my lonely life. I thrilled to the pleasure of the weaving of what seemed to me to be such angelic voices; in my pure white choir gown, I took pride in being able to participate in the creation of such beauty.

Because my heart was so filled with joy, I would sing with exuberance. It made sense to me that our choir leader would always have to remind me to refrain from singing so loud. I was convinced that my unrestrained enthusiasm must have drowned out my fellow singers, so I would charitably hold back my delivery in order to give their voices an opportunity to be heard.

Our junior choir was very successful in competition. I enjoyed travelling to choir festivals where we were always confident about the outcome. Proudly standing before the audiences in our white choir gowns, we were riveted to our choir leader who would always give us our last minute reminders. *"Hold your heads up, open your mouths widely, and don't forget to smile!"* These instructions always ended up with a reminder to me, *"… and Ben, be sure to sing softly."* My chest would swell with pride because I always interpreted that remark as a recognition of my ability to sing better and louder than all the rest.

Some years later, while in medical school, I joined a fraternity that was noted for its musical abilities. While practising for an approaching choral competition, I was surprised to hear our director give us instructions that so closely resembled my junior choir days. *"Heads up, wide mouths, smile, and Ben, sing softly!"* Puzzled by the familiarity of that remark, I ventured to ask for an explanation: *"Is that because my voice is too good and overpowering?"* All eyes turned to me in utter disbelief. One after another, they told me how I was unable to stay in either pitch or tune; when I sang out loud, it would ruin their own pitch. Yet, because they liked me, and they saw how much I enjoyed participating, they still wanted me to remain in the chorus, so long as I would sing softly!

With that feedback, I was flooded with shame! All of a sudden, my interpretation of reality in my junior choir years came tumbling down around my consciousness. Although I remained in our fraternity's chorus, I learned how to *sing softly*. I had learned yet another lesson in humility.

Arguments with Mother

It has been my great fortune that my family, and later, my friends, did not fall for my control ploys entirely. When my mother and I would argue, I would find a way to twist the argument, attempting to confuse her by subtly changing the subject. And to my amazement, she would always remember what we had been arguing about, no matter how deft I was in my mental gymnastics. Only much later in life did she reveal her secret: when we began a heated argument, she would write down the subject, and pin the paper to the back of a drape. Then, in the midst of the heat of the engagement, she would peek behind the drape to see what the argument was about. And so, I could not bend her mind.

Jock

Musician

I have always loved music. In my childhood, because I showed some musical talent, my parents bought an old piano and in exchange for meals, arranged for me to have lessons with an elderly, somewhat ragged, honky-tonk pianist who played in a dance hall in our local red-light district. Although my musical training lacked a formal discipline, I more than made up for it with gusto and enthusiasm. I discovered that I was relatively tone deaf, which proved to be a handicap to my progress. Also, because my teacher was a denizen of the low-life scene, a wisp of plunky, smoky cabaret remains with my interpretation of all music, classical as well as popular. However, throughout my life, I have continued to play at the piano from time to time, always probing into the complexities of jazz, which continues to baffle me.

When I was married, I discovered the "Music Minus O~~~~ the background music was provided for the piano solois~ music from a provided score. Each side of the record pro (drums, guitar, saxophone, etc.) for six pieces; the pianc ﹍ book. I practised diligently, thrilling at being able to produce music u﹍﹍ semi-professional. Ultimately, I wanted to show off to my wife who had an excellent ear for music.

On the designated day, I played through one entire side of the record with enthusiasm. As I was turning over the record, my wife offered a comment on how unusual the whole thing sounded. In a somewhat patronizing tone, I explained that this was *new* jazz, with *new* sounds, so she would have to undo her old prejudices about sound if she wanted to fully appreciate the compositions. Then I waded into playing the pieces on the second side of the record. However, during this side, I got some of the idea that my wife had commented on. In some of the pieces, I even noticed that the accompaniment ended before I had finished; I attributed that phenomenon to my having dropped or inserted a bar of music.

Upon completion, my wife generously avowed that the music I had produced was "interesting." Being somewhat mildly irritated over her lack of enthusiasm, I wished that she had more of an adventuresome appreciation of modern music. As I was removing the record accompaniment, I made an astonishing discovery: I had been playing the piano music for the wrong side of the record! All of the pieces had been entirely mismatched with their accompaniments!

So much for my foray into the new sounds of jazz!

Liver

I hated liver when I was a kid. It was the greatest torture to me, to even smell the hated stuff cooking. When I grew up in the late forties and early fifties, liver was an economical way to provide a family with nourishment, and so we had it frequently. I tried gross things, like crying and complaining; however, my parents were fervent that I must be fed this hideous stuff, *for my own good*. They even refused to yield when I vomited on the table at the smell and taste of this inglorious substance.

And so, I had my first experiences with smuggling. I learned that I could calmly put the liver, bite by bite, into my palm, and shrewdly tuck it into my underpants. I would stash the entire portion down my pants, and then would waddle away from the table to get rid of the evidence. I don't know why I didn't flush it down the toilet; I think I believed that this was too obvious, and that I would be found out. In fact, my parents did not find my hiding place until we moved out of the house, and my mother, cleaning the cold air vents, came upon a pile of dusty, hard morsels of previous meals. I had won: by the time she found my cairn, we had moved on in our dietary regimen, and liver became a "sometimes" meal that I could avoid.

Jock

Chink

One of the greatest agonies in my life was being called "chink" by schoolmates in my earlier grades in a small prairie town in Saskatchewan. I would often run home from school in tears, having been taunted and sometimes chased with that expletive. The mere sound of that word cut deeply into me, feeling like a stab wound in the centre of my chest. Indeed, to this day, I attribute a deep cleft in the centre of my sternum to the retraction of that area whenever I held my breath in reaction to the pain of that stabbing wound.

When I was fourteen years old, I puzzled over how such a word could hurt so much, and why others would use it like a knife to stab me with it. In my typical analytical way, I decided to get to the bottom of it once and for all. With paper and pen in hand, I resolutely began to look at the elements of that dreaded knife. I carefully wrote down the word "chin" and sat back to drink it in; *it* did not hurt. Then I wrote "in," sat back, waited—again, no hurt! Similarly, the word "ink" seemed harmless enough. But then, upon writing down the entire word "chink," I immediately felt the stab in my chest!

Indeed, there was the knife, the stab, the pain! But suddenly, I recognized that there was not another person wielding the knife. There was not another soul in the room but *me!* If anyone was wielding that knife, it must be *myself!* Omygosh! That meant that I could no longer blame my tormentors for the painful plight of my life!

In that insightful moment, I saw that some people *did* want to hurt me; calling me "chink" was a deliberate attempt to harass and hurt. However, all they did was offer me that word like a knife. To hurt, I had to stab myself with it. Up until then, I thought I had no other choice, so I would blindly co-operate by stabbing myself over and over again. How stupid of me! I was my own enemy, my own tormentor, my own pain generator!

It was then that I understood that nobody can hurt another's feelings; each of us is a self-controlling organism, with a built-in mechanism to feel emotional pain—hard-wired to hurt. When the outside world provides us with the proper stimuli, we slavishly set about to hurt ourselves, *as though our tormentors were directly hurting our feelings!* Until reaching that level of awareness, I was facing all experience as a vulnerable victim, having to fend off my enemies for fear of getting hurt. For me, as for the majority of people, life offered an adversarial system, against which I felt compelled to build a series of complex defences.

Now that I knew the enemy was within rather than outside of myself, I was left with the conundrum of attempting to discover why anyone would continue to blame others for hurt feelings. It became apparent that each person has his/her own requirements to hurt. For some, it is what is said, for many it is what is done. While one person might hurt over an act or a word, another person will use the same situation in order to feel good. The decision to do so falls entirely upon the shoulders of the person him/herself.

Some people still intend to hurt my feelings; they will hand me a knife. I now only rarely pick up those knives to stab myself with, but life-long patterns are sometimes difficult to change. Since I now don't automatically get swamped in hurt, I use those incidents to be curious as to *why* that person intends to hurt me. Now, instead of fearing life, I have become more interested in the world outside of myself!

It has taken many years for me to see the value of hurting one's own feelings. If others believe that we can hurt one another's feelings, then we can control one another with them. I now believe that feelings have been provided for us to colour our emotional and interpersonal landscape; sadly, they have been appropriated and then developed as weapons of control. It works only while people continue with the delusion that they can hurt one another's feelings. Without such control, people tend to feel helpless and then meaningless.

I now believe that discovering one's meaning in life should be an issue of spirituality, not one of control and manipulation; either of them usurps the influence of the other. The truly spiritual person is self-responsible; the controlling person loses authentic spirituality.

The word "*chink*" has served me well!

Prejudice

At eighteen years of age, I left my hometown of Moose Jaw, Saskatchewan to attend the University of Saskatchewan in Saskatoon. It was my first foray into the big world, so I was filled with trepidation, not knowing what to expect. My first task was to find accommodation and board. Armed with advertisements supplied by the university and the classified ads of the local newspaper, I trudged around town, ringing doorbells and knocking on the doors of rooming houses that would take in students. Being shy and timid, each encounter was a challenge for me.

After several unsuccessful days of searching, having faced dozens of negative responses to my face-to-face requests, I began to despair. Each time, the experience was the same. Usually, I was met by a landlady at the door; each time, she would regretfully shake her head with some variation of the message that the advertised room was already filled!

For the first dozen unsuccessful attempts, I thought nothing of the closed doors in my face. However, dozens of times later, I began to sense some foreboding. How was it possible that *all* of these advertised rooms could have been taken just before I had arrived? The pattern seemed constant. Slowly, it dawned upon me that possibly I was being lied to; the "filled rooms" *really* meant that *I was unwanted!* My childhood "chink" days of rejection flooded my consciousness. I felt dejected.

Thinking that my suspicions might be unfounded, I decided to experiment. Discovering an advertised room that happened to be next door to where a friend lived, I telephoned an inquiry from her place. As usual, the voice on the other end of the telephone was cheerful enough: "Yes, we have a room to rent. Come over to see it." Putting down the receiver of the telephone, I quickly raced out of the house to ring the doorbell next door. A pleasant smiling face answered the door; I said that I had just called about the vacancy. Predictably, she answered that she was *very* sorry but that in just the intervening minutes, she had received another telephone call and that she had promised the room to *that* party.

Now I knew that I was unwanted! My dejection turned into despair. Not being an expressive person, I wept inwardly. From experience, I felt certain that if given the opportunity to be known, I would be liked. I knew that although I may look different on the outside, my inner self was no different from others. Indeed, I was a *very* likable person. All I needed was the chance to reveal me! Throughout those early years, I was rarely given that chance.

Those experiences of prejudice called me to strengthen my resolve to know and appreciate myself, even if nobody else would.

Prejudices (pre-judgments) limit experience, diminish consciousness and oppose change. With both the natural and social sciences, prejudices prevent us from experiencing fully, narrowing our understanding and predetermining the final result. They make objects of us all—the perpetrator as well as those so judged, reducing human interactions into mechanistic reactions.

Ultimately, we become slaves to our prejudices which tend to control our destinies. Wouldn't you rather be human and master of your own fate?

. . . Bennet Wong and Jock McKeen

Family Secret

While visiting my parents somewhere toward the end of my psychiatric training, in my late twenties, I stumbled upon my family's darkest secret. While thumbing through the delivered family mail, my attention was stimulated by a letter addressed to my mother *from the U.S.A.'s Department of Indian Affairs!* Handing that letter to my mother, I asked her what possible business could she be having with *that* agency. She visibly blanched and beat a hasty retreat into her bedroom, summoning Dad along the way.

For the next few minutes, I heard furtive whisperings emanating from behind closed doors; my curiosity rose to new heights. Finally, they both reappeared, their faces filled with concern and anxiety.

"There is something we have to tell you," they said. "But you must never tell anyone else [which I would not agree to]. We believe that you now are old enough to be able to handle this information." By this time, I had completed two university degrees and had been the clinical director of a large mental hospital. What horrible secret was so dark that they had to wait this long in my achievement of maturity and competence before I could possibly deal with it?

Having dispensed with the preliminary preparation for delivering bad news, my parents whispered, "You have (North American) Indian blood. Your great-grandmother was an Indian! Nobody in the Chinese community must find this out, else we all will be looked down upon and rejected."

Contrary to my parents' expectations, I was elated! To have aboriginal blood relating me to a people so much a part of nature, with such a noble tradition, was such a thrill! Near to bursting with excitement, I wanted to share the news with everybody I knew. I raced to tell my brother-in-law, who was a prominent member of the Chinese community.

"Did you know that you married into a Chinese family that has Indian blood?" I breathlessly asked.

I was not prepared for his response. "Of course, I knew that when I married your sister. Why do you ask? Didn't you know? *Everyone* in Chinatown knows!"

So much for secrets!

A Boy's Secret

As a young boy, my parents were concerned about the evils of masturbation. With earnest fervour to be good parents, they subtly let me know that this was a forbidden practice. And yet, even then, I delighted in the forbidden fruits, and would go to my room to engage in the nefarious pleasures of this ancient art.

Guilt-ridden, I pursued this solitary activity, always making sure that the door was closed so that my secret would not be discovered. When I was done my self-worship, I would leave my room, and inevitably, my mother would discover me! She would say, "I know what you have been doing! You have been playing with your rigging!" [the nautical euphemism for my private parts]. Being so caught out, I would always 'fess up and admit what I had been doing. But I was puzzled how she always would know. And so one day I asked her how she always could tell when I had been masturbating. She replied, "Alice the Robin told me!" And for many years, I hated that bird for its tattle-tale behaviour.

But I couldn't win; I was unsuccessful in being secretive about it. I would be extra cautious, quietly closing the door to my room, and carefully drawing the drapes so Alice the Robin could not see in. And even through the drawn drapes, that hateful bird would find me out.

Only years later did I find the real truth. My mother did not talk to birds at all. What she saw was a little fellow exiting from his closed bedroom, with furtive eyes, and glowing sweaty face. She told me that what gave me away were my "rosy cheeks"!

Jock

On the Bridge

By the time I entered university, I was fairly certain that I was not socially acceptable, primarily because of my race and appearance. This was confirmed by the doors that were politely closed in my face while I was looking for lodgings. However, I endured those humiliations by holding on to the belief that life would be better once I got my education, a common fantasy of many minority races and immigrant families. I studied hard and made good marks, earning a B.A., my first degree *cum laude*. After the graduation exercise, I took stock of my life and my feelings. I was still being discriminated against, I was still unacceptable in social circles, I still felt alone, and I still believed that nobody was interested in knowing the real me.

Being flooded with despair, no longer believing that education could change such circumstances, I decided to end my life. Leaving my boarding house, I set out to jump off a bridge into the South Saskatchewan River. On the way, I met a friend who temporarily joined me and struck up a conversation, asking me where I was going. When I told him, he asked me to explain why I would do such a radical thing.

I told him that I had suffered too much and far too long for my race and appearance, circumstances that I could never change. If the rest of my life was going to be like that, I would rather opt out. Even earning a higher education had failed; I could think of nothing else that could be done. Suicide seemed a welcome solution. As we walked and talked, my friend nodded his head and muttered words of understanding. Ultimately, he said that he agreed with my logic and my conclusion, shook my hand, said good-bye, wished me well, and went on his way.

Arriving at the bridge, I walked to the centre and looked at the waters far below. I was surprised at my great sense of calm and resolve. I had no fear of jumping or dying. I wondered at the possibility of the existence of a natural anaesthetizing process in humans that was similar to the reactions of birds and animals facing death. Whatever was happening to me, I knew that jumping off that bridge was going to be easy for me.

Taking a few minutes to reflect, it occurred to me that all of my life, I had withdrawn from situations out of fear of rejection and humiliation. I asked myself, "What *actually* was the terrible result of rejection that I was fearing?" In a flash, I realized that if I were to be totally rejected, *I might die!* Years later, I got to understand that this fear of death runs through all of our lives, beginning in infancy when the results of abandonment are indeed catastrophic. Now here I was, standing on that bridge, prepared to jump and not fearing death. All of a sudden, I thought of all of the things in life that I had backed away from, all the opportunities I had lost out of fear of failure or rejection—fear of arriving at the very point that I was on that bridge! Now that I had arrived at that fearful place, I wondered what life would be like if I approached situations without that fear.

Knowing how easy it would be for me to return to the bridge, I decided to return to life to try it out differently. I swore to myself that I would try everything positive *at least once!* At that time, I was registered to enter medical school, and had worked part-time in the medical library for over a year. Returning to the medical school building, I noticed a poster asking for some medical or nursing student to create and direct the building of a float to represent the medical sciences in the forthcoming university homecoming parade. I tore the poster down and took it to the office where a surprised Dean accepted my offer.

I have always been a dreamer. Lacking social and athletic skills as a child, I read a lot and spent much time in daydreaming. Having an artistic bent, I dabbled with oil painting. Finding emotional solace in music, I took to piano lessons with a passion. In my adolescence, I thrilled over the Greek myths and Arthurian stories of heroism and valour. All of these stories and fantasies filled my mind and inhabited my imaginary world. But I kept all of these images to myself— until I elected to direct the building of this float for the university homecoming parade.

Once I had committed myself to the task of the float, all of those repressed images of Mount Olympus swept into my consciousness. I conceived of a large, sweeping stairway leading up to the throne of Asclepius, the god of medicine. Seated on his throne, this mythological god presided over the physicians, nurses and lab techs standing around the white staircase.

I immediately set myself to the task of seeking and soliciting all those students who had special talents and skills. My enthusiasm was contagious; great numbers gathered to work together. By the time we began the actual construction of *two* floats within the hangar-like engineering building, the crowd was high with energy. To match my vision of splendour and magnificence, the float had to be *big* and high! So we found the largest float base we could find and set about the task of creating Mount Olympus in the engineering building's cavernous warehouse/laboratory. With dozens of volunteers, the work went smoothly, and the massive white staircase slowly took shape, soaring high into the air, ending at a huge, aluminum-foil-covered throne at the top. All of us were heady with the smell of victory as the day of the parade approached.

Then, piece by piece, our dream threatened to shatter.

The coup de grâce of our heavenly creation was to be Asclepius himself seated on top of the impressive throne. One of my well-muscled fellow students had agreed to play the part, being willing to be semi-nude and covered with gold paint. As we were making the final preparations before delivering the float to the parade marshalling area, somebody made the observation that we could not cover our god's entire body with paint because his skin had to breathe! We panicked at the news, and after much huddling, decided to drape him more than we had planned, painting only the diminished amount of exposed flesh.

Now that Asclepius was assured of surviving the length of the parade, we began to move the float to the large exit doors of the warehouse. Arriving there, we discovered a second horror. The float was higher than the door! In our exuberance, we had neglected to measure it. Pandemonium broke loose as we sought solutions while the clock ticked closer and closer to the starting time! Finally, one of our more enterprising members arrived at a plan to make the throne mobile so that it could be temporarily lifted down to allow the float to pass through. Whew!

But that was not to be our final "whew." The heavenly creation of a float wended its way through the campus and after marshalling with the others, proceeded down its parade path in a breathtakingly stately fashion—until the first street intersection.

As the float approached its first intersection, I noticed with horror that the trolley lines sagged low at each of those junctions. I concluded that if our float proceeded, the smiling Asclepius who was waving so enthusiastically at the crowds would certainly have been electrocuted! I raced to stop the float that was in danger of becoming my friend's funeral pyre. Climbing the staircase, we quickly conferred to arrive at a plan for our god to dismantle the throne at each intersection, step down and hold the throne in a tilted fashion while ducking under the electrical wires. In such a manner, the noble structure recommenced its journey!

In spite of all of these awkward manoeuvres, we managed to win the gold cup for best float in the parade! We all celebrated how well we had all pulled together *under my leadership!*

That was the beginning of my living life with minimum episodes of fear of rejection. I began to do all those things that I had previously withdrawn from. Within a year, I was elected president of our students' medical society, and a few years later, became one of the first of minority race to join a university fraternity. My sense of self-confidence and self-esteem steadily grew. Each time I am confronted with new and challenging situations, I still feel some anxiety in the pit of my stomach, but remembering the lesson on the bridge, I forge ahead.

The bridge and death are always with me. They have helped me to live my life more fully!

 It may be that death is not the ultimate act of faith. It may be that living is the ultimate act of faith.

. . . Bennet Wong

Self-esteem

From childhood, my experiences of being put down and rejected by my peers had convinced me of my overall worthlessness and undesirability. Throughout my adolescence, I was painfully aware of the gazes of people passing me on the street. I knew that they were taking note of how different I looked, with my spectacled slanted eyes, black hair and skinny body. I grew painfully shy and timorous. Even appearing in public became an ordeal that I would take great pains to avoid whenever possible.

Somewhere in late adolescence, I began to feel the stirrings of some kind of rebelliousness and indignation. It was unfair that I should be subjected to such torture! Why couldn't I be like everybody else? What had I done wrong to deserve being born Chinese? Did *I* not have any rights? I began to believe that if this is what I was to suffer for the rest of my life, I no longer wanted to carry on.

Suddenly, one day I became aware of the fact that I actually did not know what all those passersby were thinking. Certainly, their heads would turn in my direction and they would look at me. But were they *really* judging me as peculiar-looking? Because this was not something that I would ever find out for sure unless I stopped each of them and directly asked them what they were looking at, *I could believe whatever I wanted!* Believing that they thought me to be peculiar, *I felt peculiar*. It occurred to me that I could just as easily believe that they thought I was strikingly good looking, or, at the very least, interestingly different. I liked that; in my imagination, I began to practice arriving at those kinds of conclusions every time I would pass anybody on the streets. I began to look up at passing eyes, oftentimes encountering smiles and friendly greetings. What a difference that made to my self-esteem!

This early discovery about the process of mirroring and its role in the personal construction of reality has served me well. No, I have not developed an unrealistic image of my appearance. Rather, I have come to the realization that I can be master of my own fate, creator of my own destiny, evaluator of my own worth. Certainly, whatever others think about me provides me with interesting data, but ultimately, it is *how I feel about myself* that is most important!

Remembering Who I Am

When I was in psychiatric training at the Menninger School in Topeka, Kansas, one of my assignments was to work in an outlying mental hospital. The position chosen for me was clinical director of a 1400-bed institution for the severely mentally retarded. The Menninger influence had converted all of the other mental institutions in Kansas into modern hospitals; the institution assigned to me was the last holdout to change. I was informed that the resistance to change at that particular institution was because of the fixed mental set of the people in the southern part of the state, which was referred to as the "Bible Belt." The staff were suspected to be righteous and racist, reacting to any suggestions of policy changes as criticisms of what they had been doing for half a century. It was not to be an easy task, so I was given the reinforcement of two other psychiatric trainees.

My first task was to weld the professional team into a goal-directed, co-operative unit composed of the directors of all of the clinical and administrative departments, including nursing, psychology, occupational therapy, recreational therapy, dietary, pharmacy, housekeeping, business administration, and so on. Toward that end, we met daily for over a month, hammering out clinical policies, arranging financing, and planning structural changes to accommodate our new policies. It was a mammoth challenge that we all faced with glad hearts and rolled-up sleeves, leaving nothing in the system unexamined or unchanged. We argued, laughed and cried together, welding an intimacy that sustained our energies for our common goal of providing a modern treatment program for all of our patients, no matter how severe their handicaps.

One day toward the end of that first month, I was in my office when I heard a commotion in my waiting room. Suddenly, the door flew open as the team of directors pushed pass my secretary to fill my office. They were animated and excited as they explained that they all had just been in the staff coffee room talking about how happy they all were about how much they had accomplished under the direction of myself, a *foreigner* Canadian *and* a *Chinese*. What they all had suddenly recognized was that I was Chinese!

What they wanted to know was *"Do you know that you are Chinese?"*

At that moment, I hearkened back to my university years when I had much difficulty finding accommodations. There, the message was clear to me: *I was being judged for my race and my physical appearance.* This was not new news; I had a lifetime of experiencing rejection for that reason. However, when I could look beyond the pain and humiliation of those times, I would always tell myself that *I* knew that I was a good person underneath my black hair and yellow skin, and that if others would give me a chance, they too would discover that fact.

Through my years in university, I began to realize that I was fully expecting to be rejected by strangers because of my race. Somehow, I recognized that I was participating in making it happen. I must have *acted* Chinese, whatever *that* was. Slowly, I began to give that up, expecting that people would relate to the person that was *me.* I had to project *me* past the outward image of my appearance, so that others would do the same.

My clinical directors had surprised themselves in their discovery that they were relating to me *in the way that I was relating to me!* I am a Chinese *person*, *not* a Chinese. I *am* worth knowing; I *am* a good person! Apparently, now that *I* know that, so do others.

> *Man as the completely centered being or as a person can partici-pate in everything, but he participates through that section of the world which makes him a person. Only in the continuous encounter with other persons does the person become and remain a person. The place of this encounter is the community.*

. . . Paul Tillich[1]

Fraternity

When I was in medical school in the early fifties, I transferred from a university that had banned fraternities to one in which fraternities dominated the campus social scene. There, several of my friends wanted me to join them in their fraternities, only to discover upon investigation that nearly all of their organizations had constitutional laws specifically excluding people of non-white races. Although my friends were incensed, I encouraged them not to drop their memberships purely on my account, since I had little investment in joining.

However, when one fraternity *did* rush me, I was tempted to take a stand to break the colour bar at this university. Fortunately, this particular fraternity was appealing to me because of its musical tradition and reputation. Furthermore, a large number of my medical class belonged, and I felt very much a part of them. So I proceeded with the rush functions, was accepted and initiated, becoming a bona fide fraternity brother.

I thoroughly enjoyed my experiences with these friends. Later in the year, during one of our fraternity meetings, one of my more loquacious brothers rose to deliver an oration. He waxed eloquently about how wonderful the experience of being with me had been, and how proud he was to have been a part of breaking through the colour barrier, discovering that behind my colour there was a real person to whom he could feel close.

While he was delivering this speech, I became increasingly uncomfortable. When he was finished, I thanked him for his praise, but at the same time, told him that I did not like being singled out as being important for what I represented. Only as I talked did the source of my discomfort become clear.

Although all of my life, I hurt over being treated as different in a *negative* way, now I was being seen as different in a *positive* way. Either way, I was different! Each way was an isolating experience. Although I would prefer the positive over the negative, the result of either is depersonalizing. *That* is what I tried to explain to my well-meaning fraternity brother.

Buying Real Estate

When I was married in the 1960s, my wife and I decided to build a house, choosing a property in an exclusive area in the city. Our choice was based on the beautiful trees, the city view, and the presence of a delightful creek that ran through it. Negotiations for the purchase proceeded rather uneventfully—until it came time to sign the final bill of sale.

As I was preparing to sign, I noticed in small print a clause that would exclude me from ever selling the property to anyone who was not white Christian! How could I, Chinese and questionably Christian, sign that? Doing so would be an act of complicity with something I deemed unfair and abhorrent.

I returned the form to the vendor's representatives who hurriedly disappeared for consultation with their company's lawyers. Upon their return, they apologized for the offensive clause, but minimized its importance. They said that their lawyers had deemed that clause to be illegal and not enforceable, so advised it to be ignored. However, it was still there on the form I was to sign.

I persisted until I received written confirmation from the company that the form was going to be revised, and that in the interim, my purchase agreement would be rewritten with the proper deletions.

I never have believed that acceptance of myself could be legislated. However, I have always yearned for a level playing field upon which others would relate to me on an equal opportunity basis.

Lessons in Finance

Years ago when we were in private practice, we met a man who offered to be our financial advisor. He agreed to handle our money, maintaining that his expertise was in this area, and that, obviously, ours was in the medical area. As many doctors are, we felt embarrassed about money, and did not like to deal with it. When you come down to it, we felt inadequate to deal with money; we didn't know much about high finance, and were somewhat mystified by the whole area. We were afraid of money. To rationalize this fear, we decided that money was commonplace and beneath us. Indeed, we wanted to have a pristine separation between ourselves and our finances, so that we could practice our art unsullied by the considerations of the mundane world. So, the possibility of having a financial advisor was indeed attractive.

When we offered to pay for coffee with him, he would scoop up the bill, saying, "I'll take care of the small bills; you take care of the big ones." We didn't realize how foretelling this statement was. He talked well, had a glossy track record of financial successes, and was especially appealing to us burgeoning philosophers of eastern mysticism. He talked of "the zen of finance," and maintained that "money is just a concept, an illusion; it isn't real." We found this notion appealing, and became quite heady with the prospect of playing Monopoly with the unreal illusory force of cash. So, we began to embark upon investments and deals with our advisor. And we found our bank accounts growing. He was doing what he promised. He was putting our money to work for us, and we didn't have to do anything except enjoy the benefits of the incoming cash. We then began to pursue real estate deals, which grew in size. This involved more investors, who also eagerly became involved in the giant investment schemes. We signed documents without reading them, trusting the sagacity of our high-flying friend. As the process developed, we were worth a lot of money on paper, from our shrewd investments; and as a group, we had use of an airplane and numerous other toys. Our advisor was our friend, our confidant, our ally, our guru.

And then, the bottom fell out. As the letters from lawyers began to arrive, we slowly discovered that our advisor had leveraged all of us into an impossible investment, and the bank was calling the huge loans we had co-signed. To our amazement, our "partners" in the venture began to distance themselves, and one by one they went bankrupt. Ben and I refused to do this, believing that someone is disadvantaged when someone else doesn't pay up. So we went to the bank, and offered to pay "our share." To our horror, the bank manager informed us that "our share" was the whole loan, because everyone else had jumped ship. Being unwilling to be irresponsible, we began to pay off our loan, and the loans of others who had gone bankrupt.

The financial advisor left the country. We discovered that a number of our previous associates were very angry at him, and there was even talk of getting a "hit man" to fix him. We were horrified at this; in particular, we realized that we had been the ones who had given over the management of our money to him, and we were simply reaping the consequences of not having paid enough attention ourselves. So we didn't blame the advisor; we took it as a valuable lesson. In the midst of all the legal wrangling, we called our advisor, and expressed our care and concern for him. We told him we didn't think he was evil; he had made some foolish decisions, but he was not evil. And we cared about him. He began to cry on the phone, saying "When things were going well, everyone was my friend. Now, you two are the only ones who are concerned about me. Everyone else wants to blame me."

One morning in the midst of all this turmoil, we woke early, and sat with our morning coffee on our front porch to watch the sunrise. In sober conversation, we talked of how a few days before, we had thought we were very rich, and had so much money, on paper.

And now, we were told that we were not only very poor, but also very deeply in debt. And we looked at each other, and said, "We don't feel any different." The sun was rising beautifully, our loving dog was still at our feet, and we still had our deep and lasting friendship. The money, which we never saw, had not benefited us; and the debt, which we also did not see, did not need to be any hardship. Indeed, our friend was right; money is just a concept, and so is debt, loss and penury. What mattered was our love and our values and our present.

And that has been the making of us financially. Suddenly, we had no money, and no toys, and no one else to depend upon for counsel. So, I began to do our own income taxes, and discovered that with my personal attention, we actually did better on our returns when I did them; I simply cared more about our financial affairs than a disinterested accountant we used to be able to afford. And gradually, I began to develop a confidence in managing money. Because we had so little extra after our monthly debt payments, we learned to economize on food and living expenses. As we were in the country, we found it easy to eat fish or oysters, and to live off the land more and more.

And remarkably, the debt, which at first seemed so huge, gradually began to reduce. As we watched the principal shrink, we began to see that with dedication, we could pay off the loans, and we had the good feeling of pulling our own load. And at this time, friends who were businessmen advised us, "Stop working for someone else, and get your own business." And we thought, "Why not?" I used a self-counsel book to incorporate a little company, and we began to manage all our own affairs from our kitchen table. And our business, which has grown so organically, by word of mouth, has been a development out of this original humble beginning.

Having lost our money, there was only a small item that I did not get to play out. While our finances were growing in our heady skyride, I had begun to be interested in buying and selling stocks. I had experienced a little of the circus thrill of investing in this way, and wanted to do more. But suddenly, I lacked the resources to do it. And then I remembered our advisor's words, "Money is just a concept; it isn't real." And I realized in a flash that the whole stock market system is also a concept, and in a way, isn't real. As I was musing about this, I was driving along listening to quotations about gold stock. And I thought, "I'll fantasize that I'm buying thousands of dollars of gold stock, right now, at the price they're quoting on the radio." And so, right then and there, I determined in my own mind that I had made that investment; instead of calling my broker, I simply did it in my mind. And since then, I have followed the price of gold stocks and have had all the emotional highs and lows as the market changes, just as if I had actually invested. I'm having a free ride, on my fantasy, complete with all the turmoil and ecstasy!

Unfortunately, there is a sobering side to the story. When I "purchased" the gold stock, the price was an all-time high of $650 per ounce. Ever since then, gold stocks have been steadily, inexorably declining. And so, I am the owner of declining stocks; I have to face with humility that, even in fantasy, I'm not much of a financial wizard or hot shot. It's probably a good thing that I only do it in my mind!

Jock

Junior Red Cross Life Saving Badge

Upon entering university as a freshman, I discovered to my horror that I would be required to take swimming. In my early teens, I had once attempted to swim beyond my capabilities in the deep end of a swimming pool. While sinking to the depths, I lost the sense of which way was up; in my panic, I believe that I nearly drowned, and gave up on swimming entirely. So this news of required swimming was catastrophic!

At my first swimming class, I met our coach, an affable, burly Scotsman who immediately befriended me. My oldest brother had preceded me at this university, distinguishing himself at swimming, providing a great sense of pride for this particular coach. Recognizing my heritage, he welcomed me warmly, fully anticipating a repeated success story, which I unfortunately was unable to deliver.

Within that year, I never overcame my phobia about water. Furthermore, my athletic prowess was feeble and my determination was flagging. Each swimming class was a nightmare to be endured rather than an opportunity to develop my swimming skills. At the end, I could barely manage to make it from one end of the pool to the other, in a manner that I dare not describe as swimming. Worse still, I had not caught on to the art of treading water; all I could do was flail and splash. Unfortunately, the final mark in the class included these elements in order to earn a Junior Red Cross Life Saving badge.

I waited with terror-filled anticipation until the time for the examination arrived. When it did, I tentatively managed to sloppily crawl from one end of the pool to the other. However, treading water proved to be my Waterloo. For a few minutes, I floundered and splashed so violently that I quickly became exhausted. As I slowly disappeared under the surface of the water, I was reminded of the time that I had almost drowned. I panicked. Just as I was preparing to give up the ghost, my thrashing arms hit a solid object. Desperately grabbing it, I found myself being hauled to the surface by my concerned coach who had thrust a long pole in front of me. I was saved!

Humiliated, I lay panting on the side of the pool, wondering if I would have to repeat the examination. Fortunately, my coach was a sympathetic man. He sat beside me, checking me over, and assured me that he was going to grant me a pass. Referring back to my swimming-award-winning older brother, he attempted to assuage my bruised ego with a comment about how each of us has his own particular gifts (and swimming was *not* one of mine!).

The net result of that ordeal was that I now can proudly display my Junior Red Cross Life Saving badge—so long as I am never called upon to save a life!

Serendipity

Starting very early in my life, I loved to read. My parents used to laughingly say that they never had to hire a babysitter. All they had to do was to provide me with a comic book; whenever they would return from wherever they went, they would find me in exactly the same spot that they had left me, avidly reading.

When I was a pre-teenager, I discovered the public library! Soon, I was spending most of my free time there, poring over books that were randomly discovered. Ultimately, I began to focus my attention on the mythology section, immersing myself in the midst of the gods of the Greeks, Romans and Scandinavians. I was enthralled with the Arthurian legends; in that section, I began to read one book after another on the shelves.

One day, I accidentally took home a volume of psychological case histories that was lying next to the mythologies. The subject was the case of Polly, a multiple personality. It took me a while to realize that this was not my usual run-of-the-mill mythological book. No, this was much scarier and closer to human experience. I became engrossed with Polly's different personalities that kept emerging unannounced. I was covered with goose pimples as I followed the course of her integrative process.

Following that book, I continued to read most of the other volumes in that section. My fate was sealed—I promised myself to continue with these investigations as a life choice. Although I knew little about it, I decided there and then to become a "psychiatrist."

Tennis Champion

During my university days, I would spend my summers working as an aide in a mental hospital. Many of my fellow students being tennis enthusiasts, much of our off-time recreational activities centred around the tennis courts, with the summer always coming to a close with an annual tournament which was a non-event to me, the summer staff's greatest tennis nerd!

I was never good at sports; worse, I was never even *adequate* at sports. Tennis was another addition to my long list of attempts to become accepted by others. However, my neurasthenic body again failed me even in this gentlemanly sport. I never developed a satisfactory backhand; any returning ball hitting my racquet would merrily continue upon its course after striking my racquet, which would swing like a well-oiled saloon door to admit entry past my person! Still worse than that, I was afraid of any oncoming ball. Any energetically returned ball would fill me with terror as I would imagine all sorts of injuries that might be inflicted upon my person; I had an uncomfortable tendency to shriek with fear upon those occasions. If the ball seemed to be swiftly heading toward my head, I would hold the racquet like a shield in front of my face. Being light (a euphemism for underweight and skinny), I could move quickly, but unfortunately stumbled often, landing in a humiliating heap on the shale. Although I could muster much enthusiasm, no matter how much I would strike the ball, it seemed to ignore any of my blows, returning to the other court in its own sweet time, quite unrelated to my effort.

Even with the recognition of these rather serious handicaps, I good-naturedly entered my name into the competition. The other students liked me and wanted to include me in what was primarily seen to be the summer's biggest social event. They probably anticipated that I would be quickly eliminated, then could observe the remaining matches. However, this apparently was not the agenda of whatever gods oversee the sport of tennis!

Wearing appropriately dapper white tennis shorts out of which my knobby knees protruded somewhat protestingly, I jogged onto the shale court to meet my opponent. Lightheartedly, I bounced around the court, greeting him with considerable gratitude for the comradeship that he and the other accomplished tennis players were offering me.

Then it began! Volley after volley came my way as I ran in what seemed to be four directions at once, usually chasing the ball rather than confronting it. When I was unfortunately in the path of the speeding missile, I would shield my face; the ball would bounce off the racquet, limply returning to my opponent's court. Lacking any speed or energy, such a volley appeared to be difficult for him to return. When I happened to be in a fortunate position to return the ball, I would grunt loudly and wind up for a smashing swing; reacting to what would appear to be a swift volley, my hapless opponent would dash to his back court only to find the returning ball barely slipping over the net! Many times, instead of returning directly to my opponent's court, the ball would glance off of my racquet high into the air, wending an unexpected circuitous route somewhere into the enemy territory. In rather short order, I racked up point after point. One by one, my frustrated opponents went down to defeat, never quite knowing what had happened! Nor did I. However, I wound up the tennis champion for the year.

Since I knew that I wasn't the best tennis player (an understatement!), I felt no sense of pride over the win. I was more puzzled than anything else, while my opponents were fuming with rage under their congratulatory smiles. For a long time, I have pondered over the implications of that tournament. It was apparent that knowing my own inadequacies and limits, I entered the contest for fun, never believing that I could win even one game. Accepting that gave me permission to be absurd and to have pleasure. On the other hand, my opponents took the event with a seriousness and skill that was helpless in face of the chaos created by my absurdity. That was an important lesson for the serious little nerd that I was at that time!

My Father

Throughout my life, my parents were always busy earning a living to support our large family. My experiences with them were mostly when I was old enough (around ten years of age) to help them in our grocery store. Because I knew no other, it seemed to me to be an acceptable way of life. Most of my contact needs were met by my older sisters who had the responsibility of primary care of us younger siblings. My mother accompanied my father in working in the store. Because he had run many different restaurants in his lifetime and was a most accomplished cook, my father would prepare all of our meals in our make-shift apartment behind the grocery store.

Father was always a kind and gentle man whose sole interest in life seemed to be to support the family. It was not his way to hug or kiss us kids. I could only remember him touching me once in my life. When I was around six years old, I had a toothache that could not be relieved. As I was crying, my father took some precious minutes from his busy schedule to hold me in his lap and gently massage my cheek. That event was so remarkable that I remember it to this day. As I grew older and became aware of other fathers playing games with their sons and accompanying them on holidays and to school events, I began to develop a longing for some kind of contact with my own.

When I was in my early forties, while attending a workshop at Cold Mountain on Cortes Island, I received an urgent telephone call informing me of my father's hospitalization. In his early eighties at that time, he had suffered a subdural hemorrhage and was undergoing an emergency operation. I immediately flew back to Vancouver, all the while telling myself that he could not die before I had the chance to touch him once again (for the second time in my life), and tell him how much I loved him.

Arriving at the hospital, I was ushered into the surgical recovery room where he had just been admitted following an operation to relieve the pressure of the blood clot on his brain. He was still semi-conscious from the anaesthetic when I tearfully began to talk to him. I told him how much I loved him and how grateful I was for all he had done for me. As I was telling him how much I had wanted to hug him, I began to take him in my arms. With a look of panic crossing his stuporous face, he rallied himself from his anaesthetized depths to muster the strength to push me away, exclaiming, "Don't do that!" I was thunderstruck.

Leaving his bedside with tears in my eyes, I felt despair in not being able to accomplish my mission. However, as I returned home, it occurred to me that I was seeking some physical reassurance of my father's love, in a form that I had grown to want. It was apparent that hugging and kissing was not *his* form of expressing his love. Rather, he had devoted most of his energy and close to eighteen hours each day, every day of the year, to support all of us. *That was his way of expressing his love for us.* Here I was, expecting him to express his love *my* way, and feeling hurt because he would not. The arrogance and self-indulgence of that sense of entitlement flooded over me, and I was filled with shame. Arriving at that insight, my despair turned to appreciation and I was filled with a warm sense of loving for him, even though I realized I might never get what I had wanted.

My father recovered from that operation and returned to his home. Several weeks later, Jock and I flew to Vancouver to visit him. After ringing the doorbell, the door opened to reveal my father standing there. Seeing us, his face lit up with pleasure as he exclaimed our names, "Ben and Jock!" To our astonishment, he grabbed us into his arms and one by one, kissed us on our cheeks! For the rest of his life, he continued to do so.

As usual, my initiative was rewarded!

Yogic Bliss

When I was a young man, I was eager to find a spiritual path that would take me to glory in this lifetime. When I met the poet Irving Layton, I introduced myself thusly: "I'm Jock McKeen, and I'm going to transcend." I did not understand his terse and sarcastic reply at the time: "What a pity," he said, and turned away from me to talk with more interesting people.

I was sure of my spiritual yearnings, and I just had to find a proper path to take me to glory. I investigated various spiritual practices and disciplines with fervour. My friends would follow my avid pursuits with humour and concern. I would throw myself into a practice with such zeal that I would not see anything else. I went through a series of studies involving mortification of the flesh and spirit, driving myself into the rigidity of the form that I was studying. In this way, I proceeded from Zen practice to Tibetan Buddhism to meditation to Yoga to Tai Ji. During my yoga period, I simplified my life, living on scarcely more than sunflower seeds and brown rice. My body flesh dropped away, and I floated about in spiritual lightness. I was peering into other worlds, and leaving this one behind. I expected to transcend at any time.

I lived alone. In order to maintain freedom from the flesh, I gave up sex, and threw out the furniture from my apartment, to purify and simplify my monastic existence. I would spend several hours a day on my prayer mat, performing yogic postures in order to work out the tension from my worldly existence. I would perform my yoga before going to work in the Emergency Department. I had to be blissed out, to groove through the challenges of the medical world in perfect harmony. I had to do more and more yoga in order to maintain a level of quality and bliss. I was becoming a yoga addict without realizing it.

One day, Ben and some other friends came over to my house to visit and found me in my familiar pose, naked on my prayer rug, with only a red light dimly illuminating the holy scene. As they laughed and joked, I continued with my yoga asanas, and breathed in meditative bliss. I ignored their lowly pursuits, and signalled them to help themselves to the kitchen and its contents. They retired, and I continued to practice the yoga postures, only faintly disturbed by the sounds of laughter and other sounds that emanated from the kitchen.

Obsessed, driven, I had to complete my allotment of asanas before I went off to work. So I did not have time to pause and frolic in the irreverent (and irrelevant) libations and frivolity of my friends. I was on a spiritual time schedule.

On this particular day, Ben had had enough. He had been losing touch with me as I spent more and more hours in my pursuit of satori. With full presence, and a lot of panache, he walked brightly into my holy room and saw me sitting bent over in a posture, with my naked back exposed. He knelt down and reverently(!) licked my entire back from the base of the spine to the neck. I exploded in rage at this unconscionable intrusion. I leaped up from the mat, and with an explosive outburst, remonstrated with him for such gross violation of the sanctity of my church.

He laughed, saying, "So, this is yogic bliss!" Caught out, I realized in a flash that my postures were indeed just that—posturings of spiritual ambition that took me away into isolation, rather than acts to join me to the rest of the world. I began to laugh, somewhat weakly, and put on my pants, joined my friends for a civilized cup of coffee and a good laugh at my expense.

And I have not done yoga since.

Jock

God Is Good

When I was in high school, I was acutely aware of how unacceptable I was to my peers on several counts—my Oriental extraction, my appearance, my bookish ways, my nerdish values. I envied all those youths with the socially valued looks and athletic capabilities, all of which were embodied in Wes, our blond student council president and captain of the football team. I used to have conversations with God, demanding an explanation for having me spend this lifetime in the kind of body and mind that I had. Since He was said to be omnipotent and just, what could He have possibly been thinking of to condemn me to such a life of suffering? If it was all the same to Him, why had He not given me some natural athletic skills, a beautifully muscled body, and the social skills that He had given to Wes? It was apparent to me that had I had those gifts, my life would have been perfect, without the anxiety and depressiveness to which I had become so accustomed. Since He never answered me, I was certain that I had caught Him at an un-God-like imperfection, and that His silence expressed His shame!

In the next dozen years, I completed my psychiatric training. To my dismay, I noticed that many of those who were consulting me were very much like Wes in appearance. They were good-looking, athletic, and very socially desirable. Even though God had endowed them with all those gifts that I so much coveted, He apparently also forgot to give them the capability of appreciating them! Their lives were just as screwed up as mine!

It was with that recognition that I began to believe that God is fair and just after all! *Thank you, God!*

Physical Labour

When I was seventeen years old, I got my first summer job away from the family grocery store where I had worked from the beginning of my school years. The job was with a land surveyor who was hired to find land stakes defining property that was to be sold or altered in some way. I was to travel with him throughout southern Saskatchewan, helping him as a junior rodman. Early in the week, he would call on me in his pickup truck and we would head off into the prairies for the week, surveying all day and holing up in some seedy small-town hotel for the nights. Although it was routine and drudge work, it was all new and exciting for me—the first time away from home! I was a real man!

Most of the time, we would drive out to a site, he would set up his transit, hand me my rod, and tell me to walk down the road for a hundred yards and let him get a siting on my rod. Thus was revealed my first problem. Never having had any experience with distances bigger than what could be drawn on an exercise book, I was completely baffled about the concepts of feet and yards. At first, I pretended to know, and would set off in the right direction, coming to a halt only on hearing him yell and swear at me from a *long* distance away: "Hey, where are you going!! I said a hundred *yards*, **not** *miles*!" After several such humiliations, I owned up to my ignorance, and he began to make compensations for it. Instead of instructing me in distances, he would give me commands in reference to landmarks such as fenceposts or unusual-looking trees. After that, we were only in trouble in places where the prairie was desolate and endless, with no remarkable landmarks other than gopher holes too small to be useful from a distance!

As a youth, I was skinny and physically quite helpless. Thus, I shuddered with horror when I learned that one of my tasks was to dig four pits around land stakes to help them to be identified in the future. Each pit had to be a yard square and deep, which I am sure would seem to be of no consequence to most healthy people. However, to this 97-pound weakling, the task proved too formidable, especially in some of the sunbaked prairie ground which I was sure had undergone some chemical transformation into concrete! I would puff and hack, throwing all my 97 pounds against the shovel, only managing to scrape away a few surface pebbles. After returning to check on my progress, my sturdy boss would mutter some oaths about the minuscule shallow hole over which I was furiously sweating and laboriously panting. Then he would roll up his shirt-sleeves over his brawny arms, grab the shovel from my tender hands, and in a few minutes, polish off the job with only a grunt or two.

The humiliations never ceased. Each survey would end with the location of points into which I was to drive foot-long metal stakes. It was a job for my trusty sledge-hammer. With a flourish, I would hold that instrument high above my head and bring it smashing towards the ground. Of course, it should have been toward the stake, but 90 percent of the time, it indeed headed toward the ground! No matter how hard I tried, I would unerringly miss the stake with the sledgehammer head, hitting it instead with the wooden neck of the hammer. Of course with enough such hits, I would manage to drive in a certain portion of the stake be-fore the boss would come to investigate. Again, with what seemed to me to be minimal effort, he would drive it home with a few blows.

Since ultimately my boss would end up doing most of the work himself or correcting my picayune achievements, I often wondered why he kept me on. Each week when we returned home, I would wonder if maybe this time he would tell me that I was no longer needed. However, that did not happen. Upon reflection, I remember that he was somewhat of a boozer, liking his liq-uor after we would finish our evening restaurant meals together. Then he would ramble to me about the land, the jobs and his life. He was lonely—and I was a good and interested listener. At that point in time, with our interlocking inad-equacies, in a strange way, we were able to feed each other's needs. I still have a warm place in my heart for my experiences with him.

Making Work Meaningful

When I completed high school, I knew that I wanted to study psychology at university. Searching for experience, I obtained a summer job as a temporary "attendant" at a mental hospital in Alberta. It was a huge institution with some eight to ten large patient residences built around an open court that was sur-rounded by a circular corridor linking all of the buildings. All patient move-ment to and from meals, recreation, appointments, and so on occurred in that enclosed corridor. The thick brown linoleum of that corridor was constantly being tracked on by thousands of patients' feet each day.

Keeping that corridor floor clean and polished was a never-ending job, pro-ceeding section by section around the circular course. None of the staff wanted that responsibility. Because of that, the job would fall to the lowest staff mem-ber on the hierarchy. Thus, my first psychiatric experience was as a floor cleaner and polisher. What made it a *psychiatric* experience were the psychiatric patients assigned to that staff member (me!). Because the job was so menial and unattractive, each ward would assign its most chronically ill and least motivated (mostly schizophrenic) patients who could be trained somewhat in the same manner as beasts of burden. As these were the days preceding tranquilizers or energizers, the level of emotional deadening was huge. All of them moved like the living dead, with mask-like faces and leadened limbs, shuffling slowly in one direction only. What was I, a know-nothing attendant, to do?

The established procedure was for the crew of some twenty bodies to scrub a section of the floor on hands and knees. Then wax was thrown onto that section of linoleum, and spread by brushes on the bottom of heavy (two foot by one foot) "blocks" of wood with long handles, pushed by the zombie-like patients. After the wax was adequately spread, soft cloths were placed under the blocks for final polishing. My job was to see that the bodies continued to move in appropriate directions, out of the way of all the foot traffic.

The prospect of facing this situation on a daily basis for the entire summer was too much for me. Something *had* to change! Some *life* would have to be interjected into the task! In desperation, I broke the crew into halves, starting them at opposite ends of the section of floor to be cleaned; then, drawing a halfway mark, I set up a competition for speed, with me as a one-man cheering section. To my amazement, the crews rose to the challenge! They began to notice what each other was doing, becoming stimulated to outdo one another. While the scrub brushes flew and soapy water was rapidly being sploshed in all directions, the patients' attention became focused and a light began to glow in their eyes. My cheery exhortations and frantic energy became met by their own, and for the first time ever, they acknowledged one another first with glances, followed by sounds, then finally, *actual words!*

My excitement stimulated my creativity even further! After getting the floors clean in record time with exuberant pleasure, I proposed that the crews be opposing teams with their wooden blocks that could bump into one another much like bumper cars. They took to that suggestion like ducks to water! Moving rapidly, they bumped into one another's blocks with whoops and hollers, all the while polishing the floor. More important—*they were actually coming present, making contact with one another!*

Over that summer, I grew very attached to my "crew." Through them, I learned that there are no boring jobs; I create my own boredom when I am not present and lack contact.

Brief Therapy

I recall one of the briefest therapeutic interventions that I participated in when I was a therapist. A sixteen-year-old girl was referred to me because of depression; she was socially isolated, a real loner. At the initial interview, I was appalled by her presentation of herself. She was overweight, sloppy and smelly; her hair was unkempt, dirty and dishevelled. While conversing, she had an unsavoury habit of picking her nose and scratching all parts of her body, including her armpits, crotch and under her breasts. At the same time, she would cough, hack and spit without covering her mouth. Rarely had I been subjected to such a repugnant social encounter!

"I don't seem able to make friends," she would say in a whining, victimy voice while hacking up a mouthful of sputum that had to be swallowed. "The other kids always seem to avoid me and they never ask me to visit their homes and to study with them. I never have any boyfriends."

My psychiatric persona wanted to be compassionate and accepting of this unfortunate creature sitting in front of me; however, my personal self was overcome with a repulsion that I could scarcely hide. I decided to go with my personal self. "It's no wonder that you have no friends!" I sputtered. "I can hardly remain in your presence myself!"

She was shocked! "What do you mean?" she asked incredulously. So, I carefully described to her my observations about her sloppiness, her smelliness, her dirtiness, and her unpleasant personal habits that she had displayed in the brief time that she had been with me. "As a matter of fact," I concluded, "If I were in your class at school, I too would avoid you like the plague!"

Not wanting to leave her with the idea that she was *wrong*, or that she would have to change just because of my own personal tastes, I quickly pointed out that these judgments were my own, and not necessarily universal truths. However, I wanted her to know that perhaps such a reaction was what motivated her peers to give her much space. In other words, she did not have to change in order to please others; however, whatever way she decided to be would always have a consequence. She herself would have to decide which of the consequences she wanted.

In order to drive home my point, I told her that since I was personally not prepared to tolerate being in the same room with her in such a condition, any future contacts should be with another psychiatrist who could be more accepting. I told her to go home, think about what I had said, and return for one more appointment. At that time, I said, I would help her to find help from somebody who was a much bigger person than myself. She agreed.

The next week, I hardly recognized the person who returned to my office! Sitting before me was a very self-possessed, clean, beautiful young woman. Her hair was clean, her clothes neat and tastefully selected; her behaviour was appropriate and refined. Her voice was strong and full of joy, completely lacking in whine or complaint. "This has been the happiest week of my life!" she declared. "The other girls have welcomed me into their company, and even into their homes. I now have friends who seem to like me!"

I was full of congratulatory remarks. But more than that, I was astonished. I asked her for the details of what had happened to account for such a total metamorphosis that I believed I was witnessing. She said, "It was what you pointed out to me about myself. I went home and looked in a mirror and saw everything that you had said was true. I had never known that before, I guess because I was too busy feeling sorry for myself. Now that I knew it, I set about to clean up my act. Within a few days, other kids started paying attention to me, and even wanted me to be with them. One girl even asked me to study with her in her home. All week, I was so happy and excited that people could like me! Now I know that I don't need to see a psychiatrist at all."

Upon leaving my office, this happy young woman asked me a simple question: "I wonder why nobody told me this about myself before?" I replied, "Because they didn't want to hurt your feelings." How often in life with people we love do we withhold our feedback out of fear that the recipient will suffer from hurt feelings! This is such a needless tragedy, especially when it is understood that *nobody ever hurts another's feelings—each of us only hurts ourselves in response to what others say. We all only hurt our own feelings!* Believing otherwise keeps us helpless victims, forever guarded and defended. We then deprive ourselves of valuable feedback and information.

Tricked Into Awareness

When I was first leading workshops with Ben, I felt quite insecure and inadequate. He had been working in the field for some twenty years, and was already a master at group leading. Here I was, a fresh medical graduate, full of ideals, but short on experience and know-how, trying to co-lead with an accomplished maestro. And so I took on the mundane tasks of leading the group, leaving the elegant operations to my senior partner. One task I took on was to count the number of people in the room and announce to Ben when we could start the group.

One day, I was dutifully counting heads, when I heard a voice from the floor. Ben was lying on his back, staring at the ceiling, and in his quiet derision, he said, "You don't have to do that!"

"What do you mean?" I replied.

"If you are sensitive and open, you will be able to instantly feel how many people are in the room. For example, in this group, there are now twenty-two people present." I finished my counting, and discovered that his count was precise.

Humbled and amazed, I thought, "I don't know if I'll ever become so sensitive as this." But I determined to try. So, for each group we began, I would first try to feel how many people were there, and then would check my impression with a standard counting approach. After a year or so of this, I announced to Ben, "I think I'm finally getting it."

"What are you talking about?" he asked. I told him how I had been working to master his skill of feeling how many people are in a room.

He laughed uproariously. "I can't do that!" he jeered.

"But I remember when you gave me the accurate figure while you were lying on the floor that day!" I protested.

"I tricked you. I got up and quickly counted when you weren't looking, and then laid back before I spoke to you."

And so, I had been tricked. But I had also believed that something was possible, and had practiced it diligently. And remarkably, I have become quite adept at estimating the number of people in a room at a glance.

Explain that!

Jock

Matajura wanted to become a great swordsman, but his father said he wasn't quick enough and could never learn. So Matajura went to the famous dueller Banzo, and asked to become his pupil. 'How long will it take me to become a master?' he asked. 'Suppose I become your servant, to be with you every minute; how long?'

'Ten years,' said Banzo.

'My father is getting old. Before ten years have passed I will have to return home to take care of him. Suppose I work twice as hard; how long will it take me?'

'Thirty years,' said Banzo.

'How is that?' asked Matajura. 'First you say ten years. Then when I offer to work twice as hard, you say it will take three times as long. Let me make myself clear: I will work unceasingly: no hardship will be too much. How long will it take?'

'Seventy years,' said Banzo. 'A pupil in such a hurry learns slowly.'

. . . Zen tale[2]

Keeping Up with Crime

In the 1960s, when I was in the private practice of psychiatry, I specialized in the problems of youth. Through the corrections system, many were referred to me who were diagnosed as suffering from "behaviour disorders" and "delinquency." Although it was very experimental at that time, my preferred approach of treatment was group therapy, with approximately a dozen people in each group. My greatest problem was in establishing some credibility with many of the young men who were deeply steeped in crime. They believed that they had seen and experienced it all—all of the worst kinds of possible crimes against persons and property. How could they possibly have any confidence in me, the "good" boy who had always done well at school and had never so much as spit on the sidewalk, let alone challenge the authority of any teacher!

As an opening gambit in one newly started group of especially hardened young criminals, I asked for a round of introductions of the participants. This was an especially unruly group; many of them had brought bottles of beer to the office session, which I had had some difficulty in controlling. They were also unusually voluble in their boisterous, rebellious way, and yet very affable.

The introductions began. The first participant chose to report on his criminal behaviour; this proved to be a rather unfortunate turn of events because it stirred the competitive juices within the breasts of all of the fellow members. Each succeeding person seemed to have a more horrendous personal story of his criminal life. We began to hear about beatings and rape, pillage and plunder, escalating in intensity as one story followed another.

On the positive side, all of their boasting and bravado served the useful purpose of revealing much about each of them. Also, they very quickly established a team-like sense of camaraderie and acceptance—sort of comrades-in-crime. Nobody was without taint. They even began to congratulate themselves at how quickly they had seemed to be able to share their histories and to trust one another. At a critical point in their insightfulness, they realized that this sense of inclusion in the group was achieved through their own readiness to be open about their past crimes. Then, they suddenly realized that everyone had participated—*everyone but me!* All of their eyes swivelled in my direction. They were silent, but their arched eyebrows very clearly spoke: *"What about you?"*

I cleared my throat while I rapidly tried to think about the worst crime that I had committed to that date. The incident that was most guilt-provoking for me gradually came to consciousness. When I was about 9 years old, while walking down an alley behind a local movie theatre, my eyes discovered a roll of theatre tickets in their rubbish. I was astounded with the possibility of life-long admissions into movies! I scooped up the roll of tickets and secreted them back home. At my earliest opportunity, I tore off one of the tickets and went to the theatre. At the door, I handed it to the ticket-taker and was allowed in to settle myself in comfort in the front row. However, within a few minutes an usher found me, flashed a light in my face and asked me to come to the foyer. There she showed me the ticket I had used for entry, explaining that it was not the right colour *for that day!* I was caught at my crime; lowering my eyes, I was flooded with a shame that was even evident during my confession to my group of criminals! They were silent.

Raising my eyes to face them, I was surprised at reading their silence. On all of their faces, they registered incredulity. Was that *all* I could come up with? Was that my biggest crime? Following their graphic stories of robberies, rape and violence, my little tale of larceny and swindle seemed puny indeed!

I waited with bated breathe to receive their feedback. The silence was broken with explosive laughter and expletives of derision: "You gotta be kidding! Is *that* the worst thing you've done? What kind of wimp are you?" Nevertheless, they seemed to appreciate my earnest effort to 'fess up, and made room for me in their hearts. They accepted me as their wimp leader.

Cowardice

I am a coward. Throughout my life, I have always feared and avoided violence. It has taken considerable effort for me to come to terms with what I identified as my cowardice, As a young boy, I was never physically punished at home. I was physically puny and emotionally timid. On the school ground, I would not join in with rough and tumble games, preferring instead to stay inside and read books. Consequently, I was hopeless at sports and was unable to stand up for myself when challenged by physical force. As a result, I learned how to be always alert to avoid confrontation, and how to think and talk quickly when it was unavoidable. My motto was to "make friends, not war." The strategy certainly worked; I only had one physical fight in my life, at eleven years of age—a mild tussle on the school grounds at recess. My cowardice served me well, necessitating the development of my mental agility and social skills. However, throughout my life, I remained handicapped in situations calling for physical force.

Given my lack of physical prowess, it seemed strange that I should find myself attracted to the emotionally ill, especially at a time in history before chemical restraints such as tranquilizers. As a late adolescent entering a mental hospital for the first time, I was filled with terror over my imagined need to be physically overpowering. As if to test me by fire, my first assignment as an "attendant" was to the ward for the "criminally insane." Without any preparation, I was placed in the day room to help the other staff keep order; here, some fifty chronically ill milled about in endless disorder, talking to themselves and often gesticulating wildly. To them, I must have appeared a pathetic figure, skinny and terrified, with my back against the wall. It took all of my will to stick it out—which I did.

My anxiety became highest in the section of the seclusion rooms. Here, in private, unfurnished, bare rooms resided the most violent patients in the entire hospital. Behind heavy double-locked doors, nude and isolated, these poor souls had to be toileted, fed and attended to at regular intervals. I was taught how to unlock a door with my foot propped against it and my shoulder in readiness for what would sometimes be a violent charge by the patient attempting to escape—as though my fragile frame could withstand such an explosion! However, over some eight summers working in such conditions, I developed a confidence that even the most crazed would not hurt me as long as I remained in touch with them with my caring.

One day years later, while in psychiatric training, in charge of an admission ward at the Topeka State Hospital, I received an emergency call to come to the ward immediately. Upon arrival, I learned that Joe, one of the most violent patients, had run amok. Through a lifetime of epileptic seizures, this particular young man had developed a most muscular body befitting the likes of a "Rocky" Stallone! In those days preceding tranquilizers, controlling his concomitant psychotic behaviour proved to be a difficult task. Fortunately, in spite of his irrational impulses, he and I had managed to make some meaningful contact.

On this particular day, he had gone berserk. As I entered the ward, I immediately ascertained that this was a serious situation. A general alarm had summoned over a dozen male nurses who had managed to hurl him stark naked into a seclusion room. However, with his Herculean strength, he had managed to tear out an iron bar from the window and with it, was attacking the impenetrable, doubly locked door! All of the accumulated nursing manpower had to place their shoulders and bodies on the outside of the door to keep him in. Inside, he was demolishing the room, screaming that he would kill the first person he could get his hands on!

As I scurried toward that room, to my horror, the bodies of all of our protective manpower separated like the Red Sea, creating a path for me to be swept up to the door that was straining from the battering within. Peering through the small observation window, I was taken aback by what I saw. Joe stood naked in the middle of the small room, clutching the bar that he had wrested from the window with superhuman force, his fists and face filled with hate and anger as he screamed threats at us *and against himself!* Within a few seconds, I decided that he would have to be physically restrained; so within moments, the door's double locks were unlocked and the door swung open. To this day, I do not believe that this was the scenario I had in mind—my frail self at the open door facing that thunderous rage, with a phalanx of able-bodied men *behind* me! Nevertheless, *there I was!*

Joe was now spitting invectives at me, threateningly waving his iron bar from the centre of the small room. Calling to mind all of the close and meaningful times that we had previously shared, I peered into his eyes in search of the little boy within, the one whose hurt I had come to know. "I'm going to kill you!" he screamed. "No, you're not," I said, with as much conviction as I could muster, based on my previous connection with him rather than on the pathetic amount of power that my small body could generate. Really believing what I was saying, I firmly held out my hand and made a step toward him: "You are going to give me that bar!" Those eyes—those hurt, angry eyes that at first challenged me—now bore deeply into me. Then, somewhere through a deep well of hate, some miraculous connection was made! Tears began to well up in his eyes, growing to flood onto his cheeks, accompanied by deep, heaving sobs. Dropping the iron bar, he collapsed to the floor, into my arms. Together, we both wept.

To this day, I feel grateful for my cowardice. At no time do I react with an impulse to overpower or attack, even when my life has been threatened. Instead, I have had to learn how to think and move quickly, always remaining alert to what is going on around me. I operate from the belief that nobody really wants to hurt the *person* me. Rather, many have made an object of me, representing me as some hated person in their past. My salvation lies not in my physical power, but rather, in the strength of my very presence. The stronger that I can express *me*, the less able is the other person to make me into an enemy!

 Self-affirmation, if it is done in spite of the threat of nonbeing, is the courage to be. But it is not the courage to be as oneself, it is the 'courage to be as a part.'

. . . Paul Tillich[3]

Cool Head

One day, Sid, a sixteen-year-old adolescent that I had been seeing for several months, came for a session, obviously distressed. Once my office door was closed, he pulled out a pistol, aimed it at me from across the desk, and said, "I'm going to kill you!" Having always had a good working relationship with him, I at first thought that he was kidding! "Come on, Sid, don't fool around; the gun is obviously not loaded," I said with disbelief. With a sour look, Sid opened the pistol to show that the pistol was indeed loaded, then re-aimed it at my head.

Looking down the barrel of that loaded pistol, I became *very* calm and cool, even though many streams of thought began to run concurrently through my brain. One stream was a concern for my wife and two sons—had I bought enough life insurance? Would the boys grow up O.K. without a father's presence? Another stream was a concern for Sid—if he shot me, would he suffer from guilt when he came to his senses? Would he be incarcerated for life? He was too young to ruin his life in this way. Another concern was for my colleagues in the office—would they be able to find a replacement for me, to help pay the rent? Another was for my other patients—would they freak out over losing somebody with whom they were finally developing some trust?

These streams of ideas ran *concurrently* rather than serially as I would have expected. At the very same time, I was busy assessing what I could do in these present circumstances. "Plan A," my initial reaction, was to leap upon Sid and wrestle the gun from his hands. However, having seen such struggles on television, it seemed that the gun would always accidentally go off, killing one or the other of the protagonists. Thus I quickly dispensed with *that* as a possible recourse!

However, what if I could quickly grab the gun out of his hand and remove it from the office by throwing it out the window? While constantly talking to Sid in order to keep his attention, I casually (as casual as any prey could possibly be) went to the window in order to open it in preparation for "Plan B." As I did so, I glanced out of my seventh floor window to the parking lot below. Not understanding the workings of pistols, the thought occurred to me that if the gun were to fall near some innocent bystander, it might go off on impact and injure somebody! Erase "Plan B."

All the while that Plans A and B were being formulated and dismissed, all of the other streams of concern were running through my now super-cool brain. I remember thinking to myself how surprised I was with myself. I would have imagined that I would have completely disintegrated, yet I knew with some certainty that losing control would have been disastrous for both Sid and myself. Instead, everything *did* seem to slow down, just as other people have reported in dangerous and life-threatening situations.

My psychiatric training helped me to understand that Sid did not really want to kill *me*. No, he was carrying around a heap of anger and vengeance for some other authority figure in his life, probably his father who had abused him in his childhood. Having lost the boundaries between the past and the present, between himself and others, it was as though Sid was attending a movie in which I was the screen. On this screen (me!) he was projecting all those hated and feared figures from the past. Like a slide show, these figures kept changing—click, click, click! I knew that one of those clicks would bring up the image that the gun's bullet was meant for. My task was to become as *real* as I could be. So long as I was identifiable as myself, Sid could not project the click upon me, and I would continue to be safe.

Knowing what I did about the mental act of projection and transference, I came forward with all of my energy in as many ways as I could. I talked to Sid about my family, my hopes and fears, my plans for the future, my interest in music and hobbies; at the same time, I asked him about his. I made the interaction as personal as I knew how, believing that my life depended upon it. Throughout, Sid aimed the gun at my face and looked deeply into my eyes, as though looking for any signs of deceit.

For an hour, the scene remained basically the same. Both of us were remaining cool. However, my next patient was now due to arrive, and I began to become concerned for her. Without thinking, I told Sid about my concern, asking him for permission to go out into the waiting room to explain that I was delayed. To my surprise, he said "O.K.," waving me out the door with his pistol while reminding me that if I tricked him, he would be coming out after me. So out I went.

When I got out to the general office area and the waiting room, I knew that I had to ultimately return to Sid and his loaded pistol, or he might panic and hurt himself or other innocent bystanders in our office. In the few minutes that I believed I had, I desperately looked around for help. I couldn't call upon the other patients waiting for their appointments. The other psychiatrists were occupied in their offices. The receptionists were busy maintaining order in the front office, and I couldn't talk to them without the waiting patients hearing and possibly creating panic. The only person off by herself was a records typist; quickly stepping behind her while she typed, I said, "Don't panic. Sid is sitting with me in my office, pointing a loaded pistol at my head and threatening to shoot me." At this point, the typist froze with her fingers still on her keyboard, but still she listened. "Tell the other psychiatrists and phone the police to come, but ask them not to use their sirens. Clear out the office of patients. When the police arrive, tell them to wait outside of my office and intercom me in my office. Now, I have to return to Sid immediately. Please don't panic. Goodbye." And I left without a word or sound from her.

Returning quickly to my office, I resumed my position behind my desk, conscious of the pistol that followed my head as I entered. Then, again, I focused on being real. After some time that seemed like an eternity (later, I calculated about twelve minutes), my intercom rang. Getting a nod of approval from Sid, I answered it. The voice of a police officer said, "We're in position as you requested. What do you want us to do now?" "O.K.," I said, "I'll be right out." Hanging up the phone and turning to Sid, I explained that my next patient was concerned about further delays, so I wanted to go out to speak to her. Again, Sid agreed, reminding me about the gun.

Stepping out into the waiting room, I saw that the office had been quickly converted as in a state of siege, with police hidden behind the file cabinets and furniture. One police officer was immediately by my side. Realizing that Sid might freak out entirely if a uniformed officer were to enter the room, I surprised myself hearing myself say with authority, "I'll return to the room; you count to ten and follow me in. I'll grab the pistol, and throw it to you so that nobody will be hurt." The officer nodded in agreement, and in a few moments, the plan was executed in that exact order.

The only uncomfortable fact left over from that incident was a police report sent to me a few weeks later; a ballistics expert had examined the pistol, reporting that it indeed was lethal and loaded, and that the safety guard was an old, ineffective type that would mean the gun could have easily misfired with any slight jiggle. And I had thrown it across the room!

Sid was sent to a mental hospital for several months, phoning me from time to time. When he was released, both he and his hospital psychiatrists wondered whether I would continue to see him again. I did, and am happy to report that, to my knowledge, he has continued to do well.

Through such experiences as this, I continue to feel stronger in my belief that no *person* will ever hurt another *person*. In order to attack or kill, we must first make an *object* of the *other*. That is why, as a nation, we spend so much time and money teaching our soldiers how to make enemies of opposition. And it explains why people who "love" one another so much can sink into hurting one another so much.

> *Depending on how you look at it, aggression may be man's greatest virtue or his greatest vice. If our destiny is to conquer and control, it is the prime mover. If our destiny is to live in harmony, it is the legacy of an animal past. Or maybe it is only focused energy that may be as easily directed toward making a hospital as making war.*

. . . Sam Keen[4]

Learning How to Receive

While working at a correctional school for delinquent adolescents, I was assigned clients for psychotherapy. Larry, a thirteen-year-old boy, was an emotionally deprived, socially isolated misfit who was resentful of all adults whom he believed had betrayed him throughout his entire life. Working with him was quite a challenge; his suspicion made him unreachable to us all. Months of individual appointments were filled with glowering silences; if his attendance had not been mandatory, he would never have appeared in my office. However, we both persevered.

The real breakthrough happened on my birthday. To my surprise, Larry arrived with a gift, neatly wrapped and shyly offered. Opening it, I found that he had saved his meagre allowance for months in order to afford the purchase. I was visibly moved; he had sacrificed so much! I pushed the gift back to him across my desk, saying "Thank you, but I cannot accept this; your allowance is for you to buy candy and things for yourself. I certainly *do* appreciate your thoughtfulness. However, you can return this gift and use your money for yourself."

I was unprepared for Larry's response. I had thought that he would have been grateful to be in possession of unexpected cash for his own pleasure. Instead, tears filled his eyes—tears of hurt, anguish and perplexity! Forgetting his years of cautious emotional withdrawal, words tumbled forth from his formerly tightened lips! "What's wrong with me? Am I not good enough for you to be able to accept something from me? You do so much for me; can't I do something for you?"

I was thunderstruck! I suddenly saw that all of my life, I had made a career of giving. Sometime in my experience of growing up in a family of some dozen siblings and busy parents, I had arrived at the conclusion that I had to take care of myself. My experience proved that I needed no one—that I had so much that I could easily give time, interest, energy and money to many others who had less. That had been the nature of my loving. For the first time in my life, someone that I loved was revealing the arrogance of my loving—how diminishing it is to be unable to receive love from the other!

With considerable shame and as much candour as I could muster, I began to acknowledge to Larry how wrong I had been—how selfish had been my loving, and what little room it had provided for him to reciprocate. Then I accepted his gift. On that day, Larry began to make rapid gains in his development, *as did I!*

I am forever in his debt for that most important lesson in life.

It takes great generosity to accept generosity, far more than it does to give, so for many of us it is very hard to do. But we must keep in mind that it isn't possible to find yourself in yourself. We find ourselves in others, and in loving and caring for them, we love and care for ourselves....

. . . M. Shain[5]

Forgiveness

Some years ago, I had a very strong disagreement with a friend. In the midst of our anger and shouting, I yelled, "If that's the kind of person you are, I don't want to ever have anything to do with you!" Then I left the encounter, and went home. I did not communicate with my friend, and continued to stew about the whole affair. After I cooled down, I did begin to talk with my friend again, but I had not completely let go of the feelings from the argument.

As I was distraught in the midst of this turmoil, I became very ill. I was vomiting, I had a fever, and I felt like I was going to die. My friend with whom I had argued heard about my illness. As I was lying in my sick bed, he telephoned me to ask about my condition. I described my sorry plight in detail, expecting much sympathy.

He said, "If you forgive me, you'll feel much better!"

I replied without thinking, "Not on your life! I want you to suffer some more!"

He laughed and said, "Have it your way." Well, it was obvious that he was not suffering, and I was on death's door. So, there was obviously something more to uncover here.

I began to think about forgiveness. I was thinking that he had done me wrong in the argument, and I was going to punish him for a while, before I let him come back close to me. It was as if I had banished him from my consciousness.

And yet it was I who was getting sick. This apparently was from my tightening up. And I had learned that tightness meant a loss of presence. So, I was not fully present. In my desire for revenge, I had tightened up, *I had gone away from him!*

So, to forgive him would mean I had left him, and I could come back to him. And as I realized this, I began to feel better. The sickness lifted, and I felt waves of relief as I found my feelings for him again.

And since that time, I have recalibrated my concept of forgiveness. When I do not forgive you, I have gone away from you in a moral withdrawal (a political attitude); when I forgive you, I come back to you in a resurgence of personal feeling.

Jock

 *We persist in revenge, because it is
more dramatic than being present.*

. . . Bennet Wong

Loving Is My Pleasure

When I was in the private practice of adolescent psychiatry, one of the patients who taught me the most was Earl, who had been diagnosed as suffering from a chronic schizophrenic process. After knowing him for many years, he had become somewhat of a fixture around my office, accepted by most as part of the family-like milieu that had developed there.

Occasionally, I would give Earl permission to take my car to run errands, mostly for himself. In my mind, I was providing him with the experience of "borrowing the car" that other youths were having, but that Earl's own family could not provide. On one occasion, he reported back to me that he had been driving two other patients home from my office when he was stopped by a police car and commanded to pull over to the curb. When the officer sauntered over to the driver's window to talk, all three were terrified. Not identifying what infraction had caught his attention, the officer opened his encounter with "What's your problem?" Wide eyed with fear, and with all innocence, each of the car's occupants answered with utmost honesty: "I'm a hysteric," "I'm a psychopath," and "I'm a schizophrenic." I was not apprised of any further details (although I have often imagined what the officer must have thought!) other than that he quickly waved them on their way.

One day when Earl asked to borrow the car, I asked him if he would mind taking it in for a change of oil while he had it out. He frowned and refused. I was indignant: "After all that I've done for you? . . . all the times that I've let you use my car, filled it with gas, paid for the wear and tear!" All these parental expletives rolled freely from my mouth out of some deep, unfamiliar place within me; even more so as it became evident that Earl was not feeling appropriately guilty! Rather, a look of puzzlement spread over his face as he cocked his head and stared deeply into my eyes.

When I paused to take a breath, Earl seized the opportunity to speak. "Ben," he said, "I thought that what you have done for me has been out of your loving. You get so much pleasure in loving; why do you think that I should owe you anything for it? You have already had all your pleasure!"

Those words struck home! I was astounded at his wisdom and at my myopia. Since then I have often pondered over that dilemma, recognizing that most people are obsessed with *being loved* when the real pleasure is in *loving*.

Now, when people tell me that they love me, my response is no longer the inner voice of "How wonderful for me." Instead I am apt to respond with my outer voice: "How wonderful for you!" Indeed, they are so fortunate to have been able to discover their own loving that, if true, will expand their very beings—*How wonderful!*

> *Love implies . . . . that those who are loved be left wholly free to grow in their fullness, to be something greater than mere social machines. Love does not compel, either openly or through the subtle threat of duties and responsibilities. Where there's any form of compulsion or exertion of authority, there's no love.*

. . . J. Krishnamurti[6]

Self-delusion

During my psychiatric training, one of my friends, Gus, was a narcissistic, good-looking fellow trainee who was filled with appreciation of his own appearance and worth. In terms of these physical characteristics, he was everything that I was not. Women were immediately attracted to him, something with which I was totally unfamiliar. Usually, I was apologetic for the way I looked, especially when my presence might have cramped Gus's chances at making some amorous contacts.

Training in Kansas, the geographical centre of the U.S.A., gave me the opportunity to explore all regions of that country. It being the late fifties, a time of much racial unrest and political turmoil, I was reluctant to visit the southern states. When I contemplated travelling through those states, a big question for me was which public bathrooms would I use—the ones for "colored" or "white?" A former fiancée of mine who was partly Oriental had already had an embarrassing incident in one of these states when she had entered a "whites only" washroom. Yet, many friends who had originated from those areas reassured me that the distinction of "colored" was only about black African Americans, and that other races were considered "white."

After much consideration, Gus finally persuaded me to accompany him on a drive to New York, passing through Tennessee. The big test finally arrived when one day we stopped for lunch at a restaurant where I felt the need to use the washroom. Leaving Gus at the table to order my meal, I timidly retired into the "whites only" washroom to use the facilities, which I did without incident (except for holding my breath throughout the entire time).

On my return to my table and Gus, I saw our attractive waitress heading into the kitchen. She had obviously already exchanged words with Gus, whose face was red with indignation. The scenario had already been played out in my mind many times over—obviously she had asked to have me leave the restaurant, and perhaps him with me!

Heaving a heavy sigh, I slipped into my chair and said to Gus, "I guess she asked us to leave?"

"No," he snorted, "nothing like that!"

Puzzled, I said, "Well then, why are you so angry?"

He replied, "Because she was interested in *you* instead of *me!* When you left, she came to take our order, asking me all about you—even asking if you ever would consider dating a white girl like herself!"

Gus's ego had been hurt! And all along I was guessing that his outrage was related to a rejection of me because of my race. Ever since then, I have to remind myself that I must not be presumptuous about thinking that I can know another person's reality—I must *check* it out. Obviously, my own interpretations are governed by the context that I bring into any situation. Obviously, my context has been filled with the prejudice that I am unacceptable and will likely be rejected.

It ain't necessarily so!

*We are in peril of being drowned
in a sea of pettiness and ignorance.*

. . . Bennet Wong

Reality Check

As part of my psychiatric training in Kansas, I had to do intensive psychiatric evaluations on newly arrived patients, write up histories, formulate diagnoses, and recommend treatment plans to a daily "case conference" meeting with my colleague trainees and our supervisors. As a freshman in the game, one of my first such cases was a woman from Tennessee. Though clearly lucid, she complained about anxiety and what I thought were delusional ideas about her friends and life in general. My suspicions grew into beliefs about her problems as she began to reveal what I judged to be full-blown paranoid ideas about how God talked to her all the time. It took me little time or effort to understand her situation from the viewpoint of her "psychotic" symptoms.

Organizing my material and recommendations into what I believed to be a simple case, I proudly related all of my findings at our regular case conference. Fortunately, in my colleague group was a psychologist who had been raised in Tennessee. "In what part of Tennessee did you say this woman lives?" he asked. That question caught me by surprise—I didn't know. Besides, I really thought that was irrelevant. However, in rummaging through the patient's records, I was able to supply an address.

The psychologist wryly smiled. "Oh yes," he said. "That's hill country that I know well. *Everybody* there talks to God! And most also have some suspicion of one another, especially when they are far from home!" With that piece of information, my entire case for a diagnosis of a psychotic process fell like a stack of cards, leaving me feeling foolish and callow.

Since then, I have become wary about jumping to conclusions based on limited information. As I have become more careful about this danger, I have become increasingly aware of the general public's tendency to fall prey to such errors in judgment, using those conclusions as the bases of rules for all others!

I continue to find this a scary realization! It is of such stuff that "reality" is created.

First Impression

When I was first assigned to a 1400-bed state hospital as its clinical director, I made grand rounds to see the facility and meet the staff. To welcome me, most of the staff had gathered on the last ward that I was going to inspect, planning to surprise me with an impromptu coffee break. As I stepped onto that unit, I was confronted with a sea of smiling faces and a cacophony of spoken greetings. Possessing a warped sense of humour filled with irony, I immediately flashed them a most disapproving, angry look.

"And who is looking after all of our patients?" I exclaimed in the sternest tone I could muster.

The smiles on all of their faces froze in shock. The pregnant silence became unbearable even for me, the perpetrator of this hideous joke. In a minute, I was laughing. They all heaved a sigh of relief, then joined me with gleeful mirth.

Within a few months, the staff and I enjoyed much personal appreciation of one another. So it was in that spirit that I was invited to a house party at the home of one of our department heads. To allow the other physicians the opportunity of an unrestricted good time, I assumed the responsibility of being on hospital call that evening—especially since I was the only one who did not drink alcohol.

The entire evening was most enjoyable for all of us. Explaining that I was on call, I requested fruit juices for my refreshment. Throughout the evening, my gracious hosts kept me in constant supply of such drinks. Although I generally have little trouble in joining in on group festivities, I was unaccustomedly gregarious and loud that night.

I danced with everyone, joked with everyone, laughed uproariously and moved constantly. Without a doubt, I was the hit of the party, literally dancing on a tabletop at the acme of my performance. Without concern, I seemed to have experienced a flight into mania!

Standing on the tabletop, filled with giddy exuberance, I grabbed the opportunity to teach my staff an object lesson.

"See! You don't have to drink to have a good time!" I exclaimed.

My host replied, "Ben, do you want to see what you have been drinking?" He waved an empty bottle of vodka in the air, accompanied by everybody's laughter. They had been spiking my drinks!

When they saw a flash of concern on my face, they all quickly assured me that they had arranged for another physician to take the hospital calls so that I could have a good time—and I certainly did!

Since that time, although I remain adamantly opposed to alcohol, I have been much less ready to condemn and preach.

 The moment morality steps in, the person steps out.

. . . Bennet Wong

Dignity

On my first rounds as clinical director of the state hospital for the mentally retarded, I was appalled by the conditions of a ward containing what was then described as the lowest chronically disabled. The ward was a large open space surrounded completely by concrete—top, bottom and sides. In this space milled some sixty souls, many unclothed, most out of touch with reality and one another. Many of them were soiled. The cement floor had an indented trough all around its edge; from time to time, somebody would come in to hose down the dirt in the room, and even, at times, to hose the soil off of some of the patients! The windows were heavily screened and barred, allowing only the dimmest rays of the sun to filter through. Meals were ladled into tin bowls from a meal cart and carelessly thrown onto rickety tables around which the patients would gather, some sitting, some standing. The scene closely resembled the handling of animals in a barn!

The sight of these conditions shocked me! I first felt a lump in my throat, then an overpowering outrage! "Why is everybody not clothed?" I asked the accompanying nurse supervisor. "Because they won't keep their clothes on," was the reply.

My next question: "Why is everybody not cleaned of their soil?" The answer: "They only get cleaned at regular intervals because they so quickly dirty themselves."

"Why aren't all the patients seated and fed?" I persisted. "Because we don't have sufficient staff to feed them," the nurse said.

With as much decorum as I could maintain in face of the indignant rage that was rising in my chest, I muttered between clenched teeth, "All of this has *got* to change!"

Once I had announced the necessity for change, all of the staff rallied around me. The property manager found enough funds to remodel and paint the ward, using a variety of bright colours that we chose. The dietary staff reorganized their meals and the food service to allow for more individual servings. The nursing director agreed to move in more staff so that the patients would receive individual attention, getting cleaned when required rather than just on schedule. The occupational and recreational therapy departments offered recreational programs that had previously been denied because of a perceived lack of response. The housekeeping staff agreed to increase their attention to ward cleanliness, even in the face of what had previously been assessed as hopeless.

The excitement in the staff became palpable. For so long, this ward had been ignored because of the hopelessness and despair that had prevailed. Now, as each department proposed positive changes, the other departments followed with new suggestions. A spirit of hope rapidly grew. We introduced a sound system that could play stimulating music.

The ward became bright and cheery; the staff's enthusiasm was contagious. The patients could not help but be affected—they began to take notice of their new environment and one another. The herd-like milling in the room disappeared as people began to sit and relate. Patients that had hitherto been deemed to be chronically untrainable began to soil less, and some even were ultimately toilet trained. Dining became more of a social event rather than an animal feeding time. Many began to take pride in their clothing and cleanliness, and could become involved in group games and handicrafts.

The staff were amazed at the transformation that had taken place not only in the patients, but also within themselves! They mused at how despairing they had previously been, and now, how hopeful they were for the future of these patients! They asked themselves and me what had made the difference.

I believe that when you treat persons with respect and dignity, they will likely treat themselves in a similar manner. That is the human response to caring mirroring. Contrary to what the staff had previously assumed, it is primarily a function of feelings rather than one of intelligence. *All* human beings deserve no less!

[Regarding the United Nations Organization's Declaration of Human Rights]

For in it, in most solemn form, the dignity of a person is acknowledged to all human beings; and as a consequence there is proclaimed, as a fundamental right, the right of free movement in search for truth and in the attainment of moral good and of justice, and also the right to a dignified life.

. . . Pope John XXIII[7]

Star-struck

Since childhood, I have been fascinated with the glamour of Holly-wood. I wanted to be a leading man, and I was attracted to the women I saw in the movies. I had an adolescent craving to bed a movie star, to bring the dazzle of the silver screen to my own life. Some years ago, Ben and I were on television on the talk shows. We were treated like stars ourselves, and it was a heady experience to meet many of the personalities that I had revered. The glamour of Hollywood soon began to dim as we came to know many of the famous people and discovered the emptiness and the distress of their lives, underneath the glorious patina of fame.

One night, I was put to the test. Returning to my room in the fancy hotel after taping a television show, I summoned the elevator; when the door opened, I found a co-presenter—a very famous, beautiful starlet, sprawled on the floor of the elevator, obviously drunk and high on some substance, and amorously receptive to me. To my so-bered amazement, I did not pluck this ripe offering by taking her to my room; instead, I quickly got the elevator closed, and helped her find her way back to her own. All I could think was "This woman is in danger of making a fool of herself in public. I must help her, by keeping her from public scrutiny, until she can regain her senses." So, I discovered that I am not such a cad as I had imagined. I'm sure the starlet does not remember the incident, or me, at all. I know that I don't have any regret about a missed opportunity; I feel satis-fied that I helped her keep her dignity.

Jock

Aikido

One evening in the late sixties, I was to lecture to the general public at a local college on the subject of what the youth of that time were trying to say. The amphitheatre was full; the lights were dimmed as I was introduced and greeted with warm applause.

Just as I was launching into my topic, a man's loud voice shouted from way up in the back of the darkened auditorium.

"Who do you think you are that you can talk for us young people?" the voice challenged. This was followed by much muttering and cursing in a manner that led me to believe the belligerent rebel to be drunk. The crowd became impatient, turning around in their seats to catch a glimpse of this offender. Some of them shouted at him to shut up—that they had come to hear me, not him. But he would not be silenced.

Using what I had come to understand about aikido, going with the energy rather than opposing it, I asked the unseen voice to come down to the front to share the stage with me. I assured him that I was interested in what he had to say, admitting that I had often asked myself the very same questions he was asking.

There was a stir in the back of the room as a young man came into view, then descended the distance to the front to join me. When he appeared at the stage, I took his hand and shook it as we introduced ourselves. I helped him up, patting a place beside me on the table on which I was sitting. He hoisted himself into position and stared into the audience.

I told him and the audience that I agreed with his premise that the best persons to ask about what youth wanted were the youths themselves. So with that frame, I wanted to give my new friend the opportunity to tell us his ideas.

However, no words came from his lips. His breath reeked of alcohol. He continued to peer into the audience, leaning forward in an unsteady way. Occasionally, I had to put my hand on his shoulder to provide a little extra support. Minutes passed with still no words.

Suddenly, he leaned over to me to whisper in my ear. "I feel like an asshole," he said. "How do I get off of here?"

I turned to the audience and announced that my friend would now prefer to hear what I had to say, so I offered him a seat in the front row. He looked visibly relieved as he leapt to his feet and scrambled to his seat in the audience. Regardless of his drunken state, he remained silent and attentive throughout.

I had managed to preserve the dignity of both of us. I truly believed that I had made a friend.

> *Regarding situations, making them personal brings forth the best in us; making them political generally calls forth the worst in us.*
>
> . . . Bennet Wong

Look Before You Leap!

When I was clinical director of the Winfield State Hospital in Kansas, I was called upon to give lectures around the state. On such an occasion, I was to address a psychology class at one of the state universities. Arriving early to meet the professor of the class, I was taken to the lecture theatre.

The room was a large, standard, amphitheatre-style lecture hall with a table in front. Sitting on the edge of that table, I visited with my host as the lecture hall began to fill with the chatter of hundreds of students. I tried to ignore their stares of curiosity while I concentrated on my conversation.

Soon, the room was full and the bell rang. Diverting my attention from the professor, I swept my gaze up to the sea of faces turned in my direction, now respectfully attentive and waiting to discover who I was. In that sweep of my gaze, I noticed to my horror that *the fly of my pants was open!*

In a panic, I quickly looked behind me. Seeing a door in the middle of the wall behind me, I hastily concluded that this was surely an entrance to some facility for the lecturer. As I was facing the class while sitting on the edge of the table, I had to jump quickly to my feet and sweep around the table to get to that exit—which was to be my salvation.

Reaching the door, I opened it and exited, all in one sudden movement, only to find—to my utter astonishment—another lecture hall that was a mirror image of the one from which I had just escaped! And it too was filled with hundreds of students who were also on the verge of beginning their class. I could imagine what must have been going through their minds as they looked up to see this total stranger of Chinese extraction suddenly appear before them—with his pants' fly completely unzipped!

At that point, I had run out of all pretenses. I was trapped! What further humiliation could I possibly suffer? Having nothing to lose, I just zipped up my pants, and as quickly as I had appeared, I beat a hasty retreat back to the first classroom. There, I began to lecture as though nothing had happened.

Tai Ji Master

Through the years, Ben and I have studied many disciplines in our efforts to learn about life. In the early seventies, we, like a lot of other seekers, were sampling different spiritual practices. We studied Tai Ji, and learned the pleasure of graceful, flowing movement and the sensual enjoyment of being outside in nature, communing with the larger forces.

Each morning, we would go to a park by the ocean before we went to the office and meet to do a round of early morning Tai Ji. This particular morning, in the new dawn, the air was fresh with light breezes and the scent of blossoms. The sun was just rising over the mountains as we two lone figures walked into a clearing in the park. The water sparkled in the dawning light. Appropriately garbed in flowing East Indian shirts of many colours, Ben and I were resplendent as we warmed up on the grass for our morning devotions. We had learned the sacred movements that linked man with nature:

Embrace Tiger, Return to Mountain; Revealing the Glittering Diamond; Circling the Globe; Uniting the Dark and the Light. With cosmic images swimming in my mind, I began the round, with precise, graceful hand rises. My body followed, and I stepped into the grace and became overwhelmed with the beauty and the majesty of being at One with such magnificent surroundings and in harmony with Ben, who was performing a similar rite about five feet to my right. We were indeed glorious, pulsing with Qi, the life force, breathing and swimming in the cosmic bliss.

And then, from the dark shadows of the nearby trees, a sudden horrifying disturbance. An unshaven young man, with dishevelled clothes and appearance, lumbered over to the holy site where our oblations were being performed. His eyes were crazed; he either was high on some chemical substance, or he was severely mentally imbalanced from years of wrong living. With no respect or reverence, *he walked into my space!* and brightly asked, "Do you have a cigarette?" This was crazy, because we were obviously spiritually pure beings whose lips would not come close to the defiling of tobacco. Then I ignored him and continued with my graceful Tai Ji. He seemed ignorant of our advanced state and of the cosmic solemnity of our operations. He boldly and crudely repeated his question. And so, I answered tersely, "No, I don't smoke!" My smooth movements were becoming slightly erratic, as the anger surged through me at such a crude and arrogant intrusion by such an unevolved being. But, I was determined to ignore the temptation to give in to anger, which was obviously an emotion for only lower forms of being. So I struggled to keep my composure, even as the surges of passion were disturbing the smooth flow of my ritual.

When I refused to engage further, or in any way acknowledge his presence, the bum dropped onto all fours and barked like a crazed dog. He scampered after me, and tried to bite my leg. I managed to swing my foot away from him in a deft Tai Ji manoeuvre, and somewhat awkwardly stepped away from his canine activities, at which point he pretended to lift his leg and pee on me! Now I was desperately struggling for composure. I broke the form of the Tai Ji and walked away from him to a considerable distance, to get away from such obviously subhuman, graceless, and non-spiritual activity.

I resumed my Tai Ji, shaken and shaking, and tried to get back into the harmony of the Great Unity. But I was divided between my reverence for the mountains and my anger and curiosity about such a demonic intrusion.

The wild-eyed man walked away a short distance, and then stopped, regarded us both fixedly for a moment, and then shouted over his shoulder as he departed, "Don't watch your own creation!"

We had been Zen-ned. The man was, in his own way, a Zen master, and he had caught us in the gross arrogance of self-importance in our practice. We were so caught up in how good we looked and felt that we had closed off to all that did not fit our simplistic vision of a cosmic unity. We were not open; we were closed and limited and small in our pride. We felt ashamed, and were overwhelmed with laughter at our ridiculous plight. We wanted to chase after him, to thank him. But the Zen master had disappeared, to pee on someone else's leg.

And we have not done formal Tai Ji since.

Jock

Cowboy

I once spent a weekend in Ohio with a group as guests of a friend's parents who owned a large farm. Horseback riding was to be our feature event—something that I had always dreaded and never tried, even though the sight of a horse, especially one at full gallop, has always conjured within me a sense of freedom and full life. Furthermore, since childhood, I have felt something like a spiritual bond with horses, which I had always explained as being due to my having been born in the Chinese astrological Year of the Horse. Based on that system, I even seem to bear all of the characteristics of a horse person—industriousness, fidelity, gentleness, strength, endurance, and dedication to service to others. Throughout my travels around the world, I have always collected pictures and sculptures of horses; in Vienna, I thrilled at a performance of the Lippizanner horses.

In spite of all of my affinity to the *idea* and *sight* of horses, in actual fact, in their presence I have always given them a wide berth. At best, I could manage to pet one with a rider, such as in New York's Times Square. At some deep level in my psyche I believe that I am afraid of their possible wildness and uncontrollability. With their massive strength, any sign of unpredictability would arouse in me a sense of panic. Once, in Mexico, Jock and I rented the most docile of burros, which turned out to be near dead, yet determined to take us wherever they wanted to go, quite oblivious to any signals from us. Though they were uncontrollable, my cowardice was hardly tested by the snail's pace at which we meandered through the sleepy Mexican village (and even through people's mud huts!).

It was with such uneasiness that I approached my Ohio farm experience. That I went at all was a testimony to my native horse-like devotion to my friends. Our hosts had half a dozen horses saddled and waiting. While attempting to disguise my terror, I squeaked out a request for the gentlest of ponies, which they said that they had already chosen for me. I was helped aboard a beautiful, docile mare with whom I immediately began to talk to assure myself that she was going to be an ally and not an enemy. I had read somewhere that horses could sense a rider's uncertainties, which would translate into uncertainties of their own. Thus, I put on a brave face and talked with an even, calm voice, covering over the quivering terror within my guts.

As we began our ride, our host explained that these horses were accustomed to trail riding, and we would not have to worry about directions because they would always follow the lead horse. That was comforting; so I relaxed somewhat. However, I was not given one of the most important pieces of information—how to steer!

With a few cowboy movies as my model of manoeuvring, I would tug on the reins to move the horse in that direction—the right rein to go right, the left to go left. It was just common sense. How was I to know that the horses had been (what I later was told) "neck-reined" or something like that. When boiled down to essentials, it meant that when the horse felt the rein on the right side of the neck, it would turn right; tugging on the right rein to turn right would result in the left rein touching the beast's neck, so it would turn *left!* Yet, all along the way, the horse was committed to follow the lead horse and the others, even though it was receiving my determined message *to go in the opposite direction!* What a dilemma for that hapless, well-disciplined animal!

At every turn, upon receiving my primitive, confusing Lone Ranger's commands, the horse would balk. The more she balked, the more I tugged, giving her a stronger message to go crazy, I now know. We became embroiled in a power struggle. Soon, as we proceeded on the designated trail through the woods, my mount began to take me under low branches, causing me to have to duck to avoid being swept off the horse's back (what a clever animal!). Whenever she could, she would also scrape close to tree trunks, attempting to force me off. These survival attempts I interpreted as mean and ill-willed, so I stubbornly exerted more effort to show her who was boss. She became increasingly unhappy and unmanageable with each passing minute.

Apparently being unable to take any more of her crazy rider, she reared up with some protesting horse voice, turned and fled back down the trail, followed by my surprised friends. With frightened me and my now frightened horse in the lead, the entire entourage galloped headlong through the woods. Needless to say, I had no idea whatsoever how to remain steadfast in my saddle in these circumstances. Yet, necessity being the mother of invention, my whole body responded by rising and falling in accord with the horse's galloping body. With my hair flying and my voice yelling for help, I must have been quite a picture to my friends who raced after me in their rescue attempt. It was a near miracle that I remained astride. Actually, it was a result of my great fear of falling and my cowardice at being confronted with the possibility of being hurt.

Very soon, we were back in the family farmyard, galloping toward the barn. The surprised farmhands and the entourage racing behind me all began to shout and yell at me. At first, I believed that they were cheering my heroic performance, but soon I detected in their voices a sense of urgency rather than jubilation! Listening closer while galloping faster, I could decipher that they were mostly yelling "Duck! Duck!" Being clever enough to know that this was no reference to waterfowl, I quickly scanned the landscape to understand their exhortations.

It did not take me long to understand. As we quickly approached the barn, I saw that the top half of the door was closed, and that my steed was heading straight for the bottom half! Omigod!! With what I believe to be the help of some guardian angel, I flashed back to some cowboy movie from my distant past, in which the rider slid down around the horse's neck. So, in full flight, I found myself crouching down, grabbing the mane, sliding my body alongside the neck and holding on for dear life!

To the rising sound of cheers emanating from all of the onlookers, my horse and I ducked into the barn and came to a final stop. My friends all arrived at the same moment, full of congratulations and praise while helping me down onto my shaking legs.

I had always taught that we create anxiety (and even mental illness such as is the case with schizophrenia) through confused messages and expectations; up until this event, I had never believed that I would ever do so!

I now know otherwise.

Honesty

In contrast to the belief of the general public, I don't think that newborn babies are cute!

To me, most newborns resemble little pigs, albeit some more than others. Because of this, among my friends, I am often placed in a moral dilemma. I am expected to gush while the proud parents look on. For me to do so would be a lie and an offense to our friendship. To say what I *really* think might be interpreted as being offensive. Friends who know me well recognize this about me, and don't expect other than the truth. If that is hard for them to take, they avoid placing me in that difficult position.

However, there are many people with whom I am not that familiar. When they bring their babies for viewing, my dilemma is most acute. This was often the case with neighbours. At the time I was married, it was a dilemma that my wife shared with me, although she was much more magnanimous than I was.

One day, my wife was placed in such an uncomfortable position. A neighbour lady arrived at our door to show off her new baby, wrapped in layers of blankets. Holding the baby in her arms, the neighbor proudly and slowly began to peel off the layers of protective blankets, all the while humming and cooing while my wife put on her most expectantly pleasant face.

As the final layers were being stripped, my wife had already begun the expected litany: "Oh what . . ."

To her horror, the final unwrapping revealed the most ugly, most porcine baby that she had ever seen! The remainder of the litany (". . . a beautiful baby!") stuck in her throat and would not come forth. Desperately, my wife searched for an appropriate non-offensive ending to that sentence that would not compromise her honesty.

In that dreadful instant, her mouth shaped around a gasp and dragged forth ". . . a *big* baby!," which indeed was the truth.

Such is the price of honesty.

Cocktail Parties

I could happily go to my grave without ever having to attend another cocktail party.

First of all, I don't drink alcohol. Even a little wine will dreadfully cloud my consciousness. But that is not my main discomfort with cocktail parties. I have always been able to choose to drink Perrier water while pigging out on hors d'oeuvres. No, the alcohol issue is not my main objection. Nor is the ubiquitous presence of cigarette smoke, which impels me to coast around a room like some eagle-eyed bird seeking a small pocket of clean air. I have been able to develop remarkable skills at handling those situations.

The main problem is that I have never been able to develop a taste for mendacity that is so common at such gatherings. No amount of small talk, useless chatter, and meaningless utterances will ever convince me that such gatherings have some redeeming social merit—especially enough value to warrant me running the gauntlet of tobacco smoke and alcoholic behaviour.

I came up against this value system of mine toward cocktail parties when I was married and living in a "nice," friendly neighbourhood. The main social interaction between neighbours was in such events held monthly, with everyone taking a turn as host. Having attended a few of them, my wife and I both agreed that to continue to do so would be too compromising to our integrity. Thus, we resolved to opt out of them.

The test to our resolve soon arrived. Unfortunately, it was a telephone call from my favorite and closest neighbour. When asked to his home for a cocktail party, I graciously declined and thanked him for asking.

"I guess you must be too busy," he said. "No," I answered, "that isn't the reason." I could have lied. People generally do in such situations. However, that too would be another compromise.

"Why then won't you come?" my neighbour persisted.

"Because I hate cocktail parties," I replied. "I never find anything meaningful at such gatherings."

Hardly believing what he was hearing, he exclaimed, "Nor do I! I hate them too."

"Then why have one?" I asked.

"Because it's a neighbourhood obligation." he replied.

"Only if you make it so," was my conclusion.

That event led me to review how much of my life has been governed by obligations rather than by desire. I realized how often I submit to such expectations that deprive me of the experience of my authentic self. That prompted me to attempt to be more honest with myself about my choices, *without becoming self-indulgent.*

This has been one of my major missions in life.

A lady notorious for courting celebrities sent (G.B.) Shaw an invitation reading: 'Lady _____ will be at home on Tuesday between four and six o'clock.' Shaw returned the card annotated, 'Mr. Bernard Shaw likewise.'[8]

A Public Display

As we have mentioned, a display of hurt feelings is often to control the other. Infants begin to learn that crying will bring the parents' attention; they can develop a cry that is not a cry from discomfort, but rather a cry with a demand. Often, parents will come to identify which cries are legitimate signals of distress, and which ones are merely to seek attention.

We had a fine example of the secondary gains from pain when we had a staff party on the beach. A young girl and boy were playing together on the beach, some distance from the adults at the party around the firepit. As Ben and I were sitting watching the children, without their realizing that they were being observed, the scene unfolded.

The little boy pushed the little girl, and she fell down. She promptly got up, investigated her skinned knee, and then looked around to see who was watching. She did not see us, and was far away from the rest of the adults at the party. She did not cry or make a fuss. She immediately set out to negotiate the journey over logs and slippery rocks, to come closer to the place where the adults were. During this somewhat challenging journey, she showed no evidence of distress, neither physical nor emotional—until she came within earshot of the adults. Then—and only then—was there a piercing, shrill cry of distress, with her plea to her mother to come and see what her playmate had done to her! She had saved all the intensity of the victim cry until she was within earshot, where the complaint of pain would have the maximum effect.

So, she had learned her lesson well. Sometimes, to hurt is all the power a little kid has. However, we were concerned that the mother might unwittingly participate in this game of making the boy wrong, rather than assess the extent of injury objectively; to her credit, she did not. We see that this is a very great danger in our current society; we are raising our children to complain of their hurts to higher authorities, as victims, rather than deal with situations themselves.

Jock

The End of Innocence

During my days as an adolescent psychiatrist, I was much in the public eye, striving to educate the populace about the needs of youth. I gave open talks, addressed many of the high school population, was frequently a keynote speaker at conventions of professional bodies, and was often interviewed on television. I had a high public profile and enjoyed much acceptance from those with whom I made contact.

It was probably that popular acceptance that led to my being visited by a delegation representing the political party that was then enjoying power in our province. An election was in the offing, and the political party was concerned about the local riding in which I lived. The delegation asked if I would run for that seat.

The ensuing days were heady ones for me. I received telephone calls from government ministers, suggesting that although it could not be definitely promised, if I were to win that seat, I was a logical choice for a ministerial appointment. I was told that the government was aware of my public campaigns for education and health and welfare programs for children and youth. What better chance would I have to institute such programs than from within the power of government itself?

Never before had I been so tempted by the seduction of power. However, my consistent response was that I needed time to think about the offer, and to be able to talk with my wife and children who would be greatly impacted by the decision. As usual, my family was supportive of whatever decision I would make.

The greatest influence on my ultimate choice came from unexpected quarters. I began to receive telephone calls from administrative directors of several of the government ministries. I had worked closely with many of them to help establish their programs for adolescents, and had established warm and trusting relationships with them. They said that they were aware of the rumours of the offers that had been made to me, and that they were calling out of concern for my personal well-being.

In very politically careful language, they warned me against being seduced by government promises. They were very aware of what I stood for and what I would wish for children, because they too wanted the same. However, they were aware that the government powers would never agree to those principles, only making it seem possible for me because they so desperately wanted the particular riding that they believed I could win. My civil servant friends believed that in the end, I would suffer much frustration and tension without being able to accomplish much. They stated that they were motivated to call me out of concern for my personal welfare; also, they believed that I was more of an effective agent for change as an outside critic than I would be as an inside government member hack!

I was grateful for the candour of my friends within government. I called the delegation back to inform them that I would decline their offer. Besides, I told them, I never had been a supporter of their political party, nor was I ever likely to be as I had always leaned in the political direction completely opposite from them.

To my surprise, they responded with, "That's not important; what difference would that make? The only important fact is that we believe you can win that riding!"

I was appalled. In that moment I lost the innocence of my beliefs about the democratic political process!

Inclusion

I used to work in group homes for youth, many of which I helped to establish. In those early days, we had few facilities, so we had to hold staff meetings wherever we could find space, which was often the home's living room. During one such meeting, we were interrupted by the sounds of scuffle coming from the second storey of the house. Apparently, one of the boys was angry at another and had chased him from bedroom to bedroom. Finally, we heard the slamming of what we could identify as the bathroom door, which was then noisily bolted shut.

Boy 1 (pounding on the door): "Let me *in!* Let me *in!*"

This was followed by much shouting, yelling and pushing against the door. Suddenly, we heard the bolt on the bathroom door unlatch and the door suddenly opened by Boy 2. A scuffling of feet and a slamming of door ensued; apparently Boy 1 was now inside and Boy 2 was outside, holding the door shut.

Boy 1 (again pounding on the door): "Let me *out!* Let me *out!*"

All of us in the staff meeting began to laugh. The thought occurred to us how often we have struggled to "get in," to be included, only to discover that we want out!

Such is the perversity of human nature!

> *There are really only two ways to approach life—as victim or as gallant fighter—and you must decide if you want to act or react, deal your own cards or play with a stacked deck. And if you don't decide which way to play with life, it always plays with you.*
>
> . . . M. Shain[9]

Unrequited Love

It was during my early years as an undergraduate university student that I suffered my first serious crush. Juney was cute, blonde and intelligent—all elements to which I am attracted. I singled her out as the most desirable woman on campus, and was thrilled to find that she was part of the social group in which I was being included. Within a short time, she and I became good friends. We would walk to classes together, meet one another for coffee breaks and share some of the most intimate details of our lives. We were so close that it was not unusual for us to find ourselves sitting on her bed, discussing what we had learned at classes or philosophizing about life in general. As I now look back at that relationship, which was at that time so meaningful to me, I see that I was motivated by an infatuation for her. At the same time, it seems that she was viewing me as a close friend—similar in nature to a good "girl" friend. However, in the heat of it, all of it seemed totally puzzling to me!

During one of our intimate discussions on her bed, I timidly approached the subject of boyfriends with her. Although she was so attractive, and so many young men wanted to date her, I believed that most of them were too intimidated to approach her. Even those that did seemed to quickly fall out of favour with her.

"Why is it that you don't ever seem to have a steady boyfriend?" I asked, with as much neutral curiosity as I could muster.

She replied that this was of great concern for her for many reasons. She knew that she was attractive, and she realized that she was frequently pursued. However, she found that she herself was not attracted to many of them. None of them had many of the personality traits that she knew she must have in a partner.

"What traits are you seeking?" I hopefully asked.

"I want a man who is sensitive . . . and intelligent . . . and honest . . . and caring. . . ." As she began to list the desired requirements of her imagined boyfriend, I was quickly assessing myself against the growing checklist. She continued: ". . . and musical . . . and interested in literature and plays . . . and who likes children." My heart was now pounding with excitement as I began to recognize myself as holder of all of these attributes!

She thoughtfully continued on with her list without further prompting. "I want a man with a stable future, someone interested in getting ahead, someone studying to become a professional. I want someone who will listen to me and respect my own feelings and aspirations." As she continued, she went into some kind of reverie as she searched into the inner depths of her mind. The list grew longer and longer, and to my utter astonishment, *I* filled the bill on all accounts!

I exclaimed, "But Juney, you have just completely described me! I am *all* of those things you said you wanted. Why couldn't *I* be your boyfriend?"

My exclamation broke into her reverie; her head visibly twitched as she seemed to land back in the room with me, as though returning from outer space. Her gaze returned to focus on me with large quizzical eyes. *"You,* Ben?" she said with astonishment. "But you are one of my best friends, not a *boy*friend!"

From what I now believe I know about human nature and the struggle of the sexes, I think that Juney, like many young women her age, was deceiving herself. Certainly, she wanted the company of a *gentle* man. But she was mostly sexually attracted to the opposite—some man with a quality of menace, who was prepared to play the seductive, exciting sexual games. Someone mysterious and somewhat threatening—who would keep her guessing. She wanted someone to play Rhett Butler to her Scarlett O'Hara. Furthermore, she obviously was attracted to the standard North American movie star image of masculine good looks. These were all things that I was not! At the same time, they were none of the elements on her consciously created list.

This dilemma of the war between the sexes has haunted me to this day, and has been the stimulus for many of my psychological investigations. The tension between these opposites—the desire for security as opposed to the attraction toward the unknown and the dangerous—continues to take its toll in the form of serial relationships that are romantic but ultimately unhappy. The price is high, but most people are prepared to sacrifice all for the experience!

Overcoming Repulsions

When I decided on a career in psychiatry, I discovered to my horror that I would first have to complete a medical degree. All of my life, I had been repulsed by bodily fluids—blood, urine, feces, and so on. Furthermore, I was afraid of touching dead things, and I was especially afraid of the experience of pain—others' as well as my own. Also, I characteristically would reel back from touching insects and all other lower life forms. At eighteen years of age, the prospect of facing these repulsions and phobias over the next decade seemed insurmountable to me! Yet my ambition stiffened my resolve, and I continued on that dreaded path.

I did not handle my early encounters with dread all that well. In my biology classes I was expected to handle and dissect all manner of despicable life forms like ugly sand worms and small, crawly animals. Fortunately, I always managed to have lab partners who seemed to lust after the experience of handling these abhorrent creatures. It was a privilege that I readily surrendered to them, learning what I had to learn by peering over their shoulders. Considering the circumstances and stress, I considered my first class marks to be a testimony to my bravery and shrewdness!

The anatomy lab that I had to face in my first year of medicine was one of my greatest challenges—to have to touch and dissect a *dead body!* The day of reckoning had me and my fellow students milling outside the anatomy laboratory door, preparing to rush in at the appointed time to get the best cadavers. Rumour had it that some were better than others. All I wanted was to get it over with—I resolved to dash in and place my hand on dead flesh as soon as possible, praying that I would not faint dead on the spot!

The doors swung open and in we all rushed. Expecting to find the cadavers lined up for examination, I was disappointed to find a series of cubicles containing stainless steel containers in which the cadavers were stored. Getting to the experience of touching one of them proved to be quite a complicated manoeuvre of unwrapping the packing around only the parts of the body that we would first examine. By the time I arrived at flesh, I was too frustrated to be frightened!

Throughout my years of studying in medical college, I constantly discovered that my phobias never confronted me in any direct fashion. The blood, urine and feces that I had to examine and investigate were always in test tubes or slides, completely divorced from any body or person. Only in my clinical years of study did the going get rough. Bodily fluids were now evidently part of some-one—blood could be lost, and feces were dirty! My hands were frequently in touch with both, despite all my efforts with rubber gloves to separate myself from the experience. However, I eventually discovered that as my attention was occupied with my concern for the *person* rather than the *products*, I gradually began to relate to them in a much different way.

As I began to recognize these fluids and waste products as parts of lives that I cared about, I felt my tolerance shift towards a comfortable acceptance.

Pain Phobia

All of my life, I have been afraid of physical pain. Looking back, I now realize that this was an important element in my desire to study the healing arts. Although I was phobic about even being in the presence of pain, I thought that by becoming a healer, I could do something about it. I no longer would be helpless when confronted with it. This fact became crystal clear while I was interning in a university hospital. I was always quick to offer pain relievers or help to remove the causes of pain.

This issue was most graphic during a month's stint in the obstetrical wards. I was unprepared to confront the immensity of pain that I witnessed during childbirth. I believed that labour stretched a person's tolerance for pain way beyond the limits of human endurance! Thus, I was always poised in readiness to offer and administer any analgesic I could, and I always heaved a sigh of relief when anaesthesia was indicated.

Fortunately, early in my service in the labour and delivery rooms, I met some remarkable women—they refused my offer of pain relief! I was astounded. At first, I was able to dismiss such choices as symptomatic of some underlying masochistic process, and I felt great pity for their neuroses. But when I finally decided to ask one of them why in the world she would choose to hurt, she gave me one of my life's most valuable lessons: "The pain is an important part of my experience of giving birth—it is something that I share with my baby, and it reminds me that in my human bonding, pain is as essential an ingredient as is joy. I prefer that you not deprive me and my newborn child of that important experience."

That explanation was breathtaking to me in its utter simplicity and depth. The meaning of it exploded like a bomb in my inner temple of beliefs! It took some time to digest the breadth and depth of its implications. In the meantime, being without apparent use in the labour room, I found myself given to pacing the floor and fretting, which I am sure must have been disconcerting to the women in labour. Finally, while I stood wringing my hands in desperation, one of them who had refused analgesia gently asked me about my evident anxiety. I remarked that I didn't like the feeling of helplessness that I was experiencing. She invited me to sit with her and hold her hand while she was feeling her labour pains.

During that session, I learned an important lesson in the resonant aspect of empathy. With each labour pain, I felt some inner pain of my own. With each cry or scream, I too would utter some sound. By the time the baby was born, I felt an incredible bonding with mother and child. Now I understood what that mother had related to me about pain and bonding. Now I believe that feelings are limited in scope when they are unshared, that fear grows in isolation, and that pain can be an opportunity for bonding. Now I am less phobic about all of these feelings.

I had discovered the value of *sharing* pain.

 Pain is an unseen and powerful hand that breaks the skin of the stone in order to extract the pulp.

. . . Kahlil Gibran[10]

My First Encounter with Death

During my internship on the Internal Medicine wards of the hospital, I was assigned to take care of a youngish middle-aged man who had suffered a heart attack—his first. His symptoms were so severe that he required special attention much of the time. Although he was constantly sedated and under an oxygen tent most of the time, I was required to be with him much of the day and night, monitoring his vital signs. On the occasions that he would drift into consciousness, we would talk quietly and meaningfully, getting to know one another at some deep cellular level. In a strange, mysterious way, I believed that we had come to mean something important to one another. For an entire week, we struggled together to survive. His wife and children were often by my side as I administered necessary medications and procedures; so I soon got to feel myself an important part of his family.

Then, he suddenly died! I was stunned. After all those hours of my caring and ministering, I could not believe that he would leave me! Anger and grief overcame me as I held his hand and called his name. Tears streamed down my face.

Suddenly, I noticed a supporting arm around my shoulders. I turned my head; through my tears, I recognized the patient's wife, weeping quietly by my side. For many minutes, we shared our common grief over the loss of somebody we both loved.

Less than a week later, I was surprised to receive a large bouquet of flowers on the ward. Opening the card, I discovered that the flowers had been sent by the dead patient's family. The flowers had been used at his funeral; the family wanted to express to me their sympathy over *my* loss!

 Where there is sorrow there is holy ground.

   . . . Oscar Wilde[11]

Phillip

When I was an intern on a pediatrics ward, I became actively involved with Phillip, a six-year-old suffering from hemophilia. In the whole ward of many children, he stood out for me. Blond, thin, quiet, and wan, he would not play with the other patients. Rather, he would sit by himself in a corner, head hung and hands folded in his lap. It appeared as though he was succumbing to the inevitability of death that we as staff knew to be his fate. He had been admitted for terminal care.

Our hearts went out to this lonely boy. For some reason that I now am unable to remember, not even his parents were present much of the time. At every spare moment I had, I would sit beside his mute figure and carry on a one-sided conversation. At times, after his giving assent with a nod of the head, I would read children's stories to him. For brief moments, he would come present to be with me, but overall, he did not seem enthusiastic or welcoming of my intrusions. Yet, because of some gnawing resonance within my own lonely soul, I persisted.

We treated Phillip's hemophilic crisis with all that we could. He mutely accepted all of our ministrations and medications without a word of protest—a remarkable feat on this pediatric ward. It was impossible for us to know whether his lack of resistance was a symptom of trust in us or of a loss of caring about himself. For whatever reason, over the course of several weeks, he survived that admission and was discharged, diagnosed as having had a spontaneous remission.

Although Phillip's sad, drawn and pallid face continued to haunt me over the ensuing months, my attention was captured by my duties on an obstetrical ward to which I had been transferred. One day, I heard myself being paged on the hospital call system, requesting my presence at the admissions office. I hurried to respond. On arrival, to my surprise, I found Phillip! In the process of being admitted, he actually talked—to ask for me! Although I no longer was assigned to pediatrics, the admissions nurse somehow knew that it was important for me to be there with Phillip. I smiled at him as I shook his limp hand, the only physical gesture that he had allowed in our interaction.

Shepherding him through the routine admissions procedure, I was saddened to learn that his attending physician had had to readmit him for the same reasons as before; only this time, the symptoms were worse. I wheelchaired him to the ward where he was warmly received by the loving staff. For some minutes, we all enjoyed our unexpected reunion before I had to return to my other duties.

Daily, I returned to visit Phillip, even though I could not be actively engaged in his treatment. Unfortunately, he went from bad to worse in a very few days. It was becoming evident that he was unlikely to recover this time. Now he was too weak to leave his bed. So, I would sit on the edge of his bed (a strict hospital taboo) for my one-sided conversations and readings with him. In those moments, I could detect some faint light in his eyes as he struggled to come forth in my presence. However, the course of his illness was definitely downhill.

One day, just before his death, Phillip mustered all of his strength to sit up to spontaneously give me a hug. I wept, knowing this to be a gesture of gratitude and farewell at the same time!

To this day, I am haunted by Phillip's face.

 With intimacy, you are known; when you are known, you are never alone.

... Bennet Wong

88

Fatigue

I was the first intern to arrive at the opening of Saskatoon's new University Hospital. For one month, I was the *only* intern. During that month, I and two other house staff "residents" (senior trainees) admitted all of the newly arriving patients and covered all of the wards. Under these unusual circumstances, we three agreed to no time off for that month. We covered for one another while we took turns grabbing naps whenever we could—day or night. The nurses were exceptionally thoughtful, doing what they could to relieve us of some duties, propping us up in comfortable chairs so that we could sleep for ten or fifteen minutes.

Most of the time, the task at hand was demanding enough to keep me awake and alert. Once, I nearly succumbed while monitoring the temperature of a patient undergoing delicate surgery under hypothermia. In those days the procedure was in its experimental stages. On the surgical table, the patient was wrapped in special cooling coils that would bring the patient's body temperature to low levels in which delicate surgical procedures could be performed for extended periods of time. A rectal thermometer was connected to a monitoring device under the operating table. On this occasion, that was to be my particular job. I was ensconced in a cramped position under the surgical drapes, with the responsibility of maintaining the cooling mechanism at a level that would ensure the patient's body temperature remained constantly low. In that position for hours, I stared at the monitor that gave me the temperature readings. Occasionally, a demand for the reading would come down to me from above, and I would dutifully deliver a vocal response. Needless to say, after weeks of little sleep, the temptation to doze off was high, so I had to frequently pinch myself to keep myself awake.

My fatigue was cumulative. Toward the end of that impossible month, I hardly felt alive. In that state I had my most difficult incident. From the emergency ward, I had admitted a patient to surgery because of symptoms of a seriously life-threatening situation. The man's aorta (the main artery located in the back of the abdominal wall) was beginning to rupture. Saving his life would necessitate a particularly long and complicated procedure—an aortic graft that would involve four separate surgical teams. When my diagnosis had been confirmed by the on-call senior staff, approval was given and a time was set for later in the day.

The task of co-ordinating the teams for the aortic graft fell on my exhausted shoulders. That I did with dispatch. However, the difficult part was that I (along with a senior surgical resident) was also selected to assist the chief of surgery who was to place the actual graft within the abdomen. My main function was to keep the surgical wound free of blood through the use of suction and gauze packs while the surgeons cut and mended. Under the bright surgical lights, my eyes were strained. Behind my surgical mask and gown the air grew warm and stale as the hours passed. Added to that was the pressure I felt performing with the hallowed chief of surgery, a man of icy bearing, with beady, bright, piercing eyes and razor-sharp tongue! The energy of my "personal best" gradually turned to mush as I began to doze.

My consciousness clouded over and over again; as I would catch myself sinking into sleep, my head would jerk anew into an upright position. I hoped that nobody present could see my shoddy performance! Suddenly, I was aware of being pierced by the chief surgeon's icy voice: "Would the good doctor keep his head *out* of the surgical field?"

It was like a bucket of cold water dashed on my face! From that point on, I had no trouble keeping awake.

That month, many people who witnessed my marathon performance believed that I had been unfairly overworked. I disagree. I only worked as much as I was able; this experience took me to the limits of my endurance. I am pleased to know those limits.

My Day in Heaven

While I was in psychiatric practice, several of my adolescent patients suffered from schizophrenic processes. I was fascinated with their hallucinations, having none of my own experience that could help me to understand how they felt. One particular youth (whom I shall call Ed) was particularly generous in describing to me his hallucinatory experiences. Usually, he would take delight at educating me; occasionally, his delusional system would leave me far behind as he would get lost in the symbolic complexities of his mind.

On one occasion, Ed arrived at my office in a state of panic. His eyes darted around the room with fear, as he carefully made his way across the room to my desk. I asked, "What's wrong, Ed?"

"The devil is present," was his frightened response.

"Where?" I asked incredulously.

"Over there," he said, pointing close to me. "As a matter of fact you almost stepped on him when you got up to greet me."

As Ed sat before me, I knew that this line of questioning would lead down blind alleys. "Let's talk about something else, Ed," I said. Pointing to a deck of tarot cards that I kept on my desk, I suggested, "Let's ask the tarot what we should discuss."

Ed sullenly agreed and reached for the cards. Being accustomed to the procedure, he began to slowly shuffle the deck, ultimately replacing it on to the desk top. "Now cut the deck," I said. Ed did as he was told, turning up the top part of the deck. As he did so, my heart leaped into my throat as I recognized the selected card to be *the Devil!*

"See!" Ed exclaimed triumphantly. "And you didn't believe me!"

With Ed, I began to believe more and more, losing many of my arrogant psychiatric concepts along the way. I began to crave for the hallucinatory experience of the schizophrenic. When I read that some people were suggesting the similarity between those experiences and LSD-induced hallucinations, I grew excited. Although I had guided many a youth down from an LSD "bad trip," I had no personal experience with the drug myself. Knowing some psychiatrists that had experimented with the drug, I sought their help, which they gladly offered.

The day for my initiation to the LSD experience was set, and I arrived at the designated place with my heart in my throat. Assembled in a comfortable apartment were many good friends who had agreed to be with me. My psychiatric friend gave me the appropriate dose, and I sat on a bed to await the results.

I soon lost the sense of time, so that I cannot report this with any accuracy at all. Soon, my perceptions of the room became loose and wavy, as stationary objects began to dance around my field of vision. I felt as though I was flying in an upward vortex, much as I have always imagined Dorothy within the tornado in *The Wizard of Oz*. After a perceived lengthy period of time (that in actuality may have only been a few minutes), I began to hear the clear voices of a heavenly choir singing hallelujahs! A bright light swirled all around me, encompassing me and carrying me higher and higher! I felt a joyful ecstasy near to bursting. I remember thinking that I must be in heaven, although I never met God there; instead, I just felt an expansive sense of well-being and peace. I knew that I wanted to stay in this place, leaving behind all of my earthly travails.

At the same time as I arrived at this yearning to remain, another voice filled me with the understanding that I must return to earth, where I had a lot of unfinished things to do. With that conclusion, the vortex reversed itself and I began to fall.

During my free fall, I did exactly what I had always advised others against—I began to tighten up. As I did so, I was confronted with the horrendously ugly and frightening face of what I concluded was the Devil! It leered as it pursued me across the chasms of space, and I raced and raced with no place to hide! "Wait a minute, you fool!" I could hear myself exclaim. "This bad trip is your own doing because you are resisting. You must relax!" How often have I delivered these same words to my young, drugged patients? "You must follow your own advice!"

So I let go and surrendered to the experience. I began a gentle fall through light and clouds, slowly becoming aware of myself clinging to the back of one of my women friends. My friends later reported to me that from the outside, they were able to see that I had gone into a bad space, and had physically held me to comfort me. My consciousness ultimately caught up with my body, leaving me feeling refreshed and whole. It had been a great "white light" trip!

Eager to tell Ed about what I had experienced, I raced to his group home. He met me at the door, and before I had the chance to utter a word, he quickly retreated into the house. Following him into the dining room, I was exclaiming that I had much to tell him. But he would not listen. Whenever I tried to come around to his side of the dining room table, he would quickly move to the opposite side, all the while glowering at me.

"What's wrong, Ed?" I asked.

Although he had not been informed about any of my intentions that day, he replied in a severe tone, "Go and *work* for your day in Heaven!" I was stunned.

To this day, I carry with me the question of the possibility that some so-called mental illness involves some loosening of the boundaries between the world of the five senses and what some researchers describe as the Psi state—another level of human experience that is so little understood.

I am no longer so arrogant about my beliefs about reality.

And I continue to work for my day in Heaven!

Sparkles

Early in my psychiatric practice, I began to hear about the work of Wilhelm Reich, whom I had never previously studied. A one-time follower of Freud, he proposed that a person's problems were written in the body. Such a person could only be free when the body lets go of its tensions. The idea fascinated me, but at that time, I could find no place to go to study these radical ideas. I discovered some information about Ida Rolf, who believed that the tension was held in a biochemical process involving the muscles, their fascial sheaths, and ligaments. She had developed a method of deep muscle massage aimed at breaking up these deep-tissue defensive "blocks," and had trained some people in her "rolfing" methods. I ultimately made contact with such a rolfer and set up a series of ten appointments with him.

During my first session, I was fairly comfortable with the deep massage. My rolfer commented to me that he found me too easy—that I was too undefended. Instead of having to remove energy blocks, he suggested that he might have to help me find some defenses. I was flattered by his comments, but the next session was entirely different.

During session two, I experienced severe pain wherever he probed and massaged. My stout resolve kept me on the massage table, but I had to scream aloud to make the pain bearable! At his suggestion, I breathed deeply and rapidly and really tried to *surrender* to the pain, which I understood to be the goal of the exercise. But the pain just increased and I yelled even louder.

In the midst of one of my loudest spine-tingling screams, I suddenly realized that most of my scream was a scam. I thought that if I screamed loud enough, my rolfing assailant would ease up on me. However, it became apparent that he was going to show no mercy. The louder I screamed, the *deeper* he went. Giving up that strategy gave me the opportunity to focus my attention back to myself and my inner experiences. Now my screams were only directly related to the pain itself.

When I had fully arrived at that decision, the pain seemed to disappear! At that moment of *surrender*, my entire visual field was suddenly altered. I could *see* energy dancing between all things that now emitted delightful sparkles. The rolfer then retreated, leaving me to lie on the table to experience my newly discovered world of sparkles. I was in awe!

Getting up from the massage table, I slowly wandered outside and flung myself on the ground and lay on my back in the middle of a forest. Looking up at the sky, I saw the sparkles in the infinite blue and in the drifting clouds. All around me, the same sparkles danced from the tips of the evergreens and in the flowers and plants. It was all so breathtakingly beautiful! I lay there in bliss while various people came outdoors from time to time to check my welfare. I discovered that they, too, sparkled!

After some time (actually, I lost any sense of time), my rolfer came by to look down at me. I marvelled at his beatific smile and the beauty I saw in all of the people. Seeing me struggle to communicate my experience to him, he gently touched me to dissuade me from talking.

"When will you ever just accept your bliss, Ben?" he said as he parted, leaving me alone to join in the sparkling universe!

The heavens declare the glory of God;
and the firmament sheweth his handywork.

. . . Psalms 19:1

The Pain of Compassion

Shortly after beginning to lead groups, I was joined by my partner, Jock, who wished to learn the art of group leading. After each session, we spent time to debrief the experiences we had created. I would teach Jock at that time, explaining why I did such and such, and critiquing work that he had directed. Because he was prone to romanticizing the work, I spent considerable time demystifying the process with him. In his account in this book entitled "Tricked Into Awareness" (p. 42), Jock describes one such experience.

Although I had not planned it, another occasion arose to teach him about the seductiveness of pretensions. Following some particularly tender work in a group, I was awash with tears. At that time, having difficulty accessing his own feelings, Jock interrogated me closely about mine. I carefully described to him how choked up I would get in my chest, often accompanied by a sharp pain over my heart chakra, just as I was feeling at that time. Jock berated himself over his own insensitivity, and was in awe at the depth of my pain of compassion. He again mystified the experience.

The next day, I recalled Jock for a follow-up to our conversation about compassion. With a shamed face, I acknowledged that I had discovered that the sharp pain that I had described in the centre of my chest was due to a more mundane cause. A pimple that had burst that same evening was the source of my discomfort!

That certainly demystified that experience!

> Compassion is feeling with another, or love. The escape from boredom and the recovery of passion begins with the emotion of compassion......Compassion spells the beginning of the end of boredom, because it ends our isolation.
>
> . . . Sam Keen[12]

Standing Firm

My family of origin was a peculiar combination of modernism and rigid traditional values. Like many other Oriental families in North America, we were strongly motivated by a meme (behavioural pattern) toward achievement and success in professional fields of endeavour. At the same time, we were strongly programmed to remain aware of our Chinese heritage and always warned against becoming too involved with Caucasian friends. In my early teens, I remember having to sneak out of our makeshift apartment behind our grocery store to take dance lessons that were strictly taboo as far as my parents were concerned. It was a desperate move on my part to learn a social skill that would help me to belong in the adolescent social scene.

In spite of all of my parents' opposition, I managed to eke out some level of social acceptance among my peers. However, dating was a near impossibility because of the strong sanctions against the possibility of becoming involved with a "white" girl. In our small town and later in my university town, there were no Chinese girls in sight. It was not until I was in psychiatric training that I finally met an Oriental woman to whom I was attracted.

After a relatively short courtship, we were engaged to be married. I remember thinking that, at last, my parents would be happy. Unfortunately, she was primarily of Philippine origin, with only secondary Chinese blood. When my parents discovered this, they went into a fury. In some ways, their prejudices saw this combination to be even worse than a mixture of Chinese-Caucasian blood! Not only did they berate me—they even threatened to disown me if I were to proceed with my marriage plans. I was thrown into turmoil. Finally, I acquiesced to their demands and backed out of that relationship, fearing family exile to an extent I could not consciously understand at that time.

Many years later, I did marry to their liking, and began the creation of a family of my own. After the birth of two sons and a dozen years of marriage, it became apparent that our relationship was faltering. Consulting a family and relationship therapist, one of the first questions we were asked was, "What are each of you willing to sacrifice to make this marriage work?"

I gulped as I saw the implications of that question. It was apparent that this therapist would have us both reduced to the lowest common denominator "for the sake of the marriage and the children!" I was at first appalled, then offended. Ultimately deciding that our relationship was not serving either of our needs very well, my wife and I agreed on a divorce.

When my parents learned about our decision, they were furious, in a way very similar to my earlier desire to marry a non-pure-Chinese person. Their words were the same: "How could you bring such shame upon the family?" Their concern was all for the public appearance of the family—the maintenance of social position and high regard in the Chinese community.

Although I had been cowed by the first attack upon my decisions for my own happiness, this time I was resolute. Perhaps now I was more mature; or maybe I was only becoming numb to such pressure on my behaviour. With some sadness, I decided to accept their threatened ostracism; if I ever were to achieve some permanent happiness, it might have to be at the price of relinquishing my membership in this family. While the divorce action proceeded over the next five years, I was no longer invited to family gatherings or celebrations. Over the ensuing years, I began to accept my role as outcast. Time has proven my choice to have been of immense value to me; I now know happiness of unprecedented and unexpected proportions. I now know fulfilment.

Time has also healed the family breach, and hardly any of us now remember the tension of those days. However, the lesson that I learned—to be steadfast and true to my heart—forever remains in my soul.

'Selfish' is a moral word; 'self-centred' is a location word. Although they are frequently used interchangeably, they are not the same.

. . . Bennet Wong

A Fear of Zen Flying

My friend Alan Watts taught me many a Zen lesson. Living on a small Gulf Island for several years necessitated the use of small float planes to come and go when we were in too much of a hurry to use the ferry system. On one such trip, Alan and his wife accompanied me; they were scrunched into the back seat while I sat beside the pilot. The day was beautiful; the weather was clear, calm and sunny. We all were in high spirits, anticipating the pleasure of participating in a Zen workshop together. I had no apprehension about the short flight that I had taken many times before.

The takeoff on the calm water was smooth. We were all safely buckled in. Alan's spirits were especially high; he filled the small craft with his usual clever comments as we rose into the air. Suddenly, the unexpected happened—we struck some kind of air pocket that violently threw the plane on its right side! My heart leaped into my throat as my door flew open and I found myself horizontal, staring directly down upon open water! Of course, I was safe because of my seat belt, but the sudden sight of no protective door between me, open space and ocean was a startling experience! From the back seat, peals of laughter and chortles rolled out of Alan's wide open throat as his free spirit danced with our roller coaster ride. As our plane righted, I gradually regained my composure enough to silently nod reluctant assent to Alan's assertion that the Universe was certainly full of fun and pleasure that day.

Experiences like that with Alan helped me to ride more easily with Nature, but it took me a little more time to *celebrate* such unpredictabilities. Alan persevered at trying to teach me. Once, I was flying to the small island as a solo passenger in the tiny aircraft. The approach to the landing wharf was an especially tricky one, necessitating a sideswiping bank as we swooped around a corner and had to drop suddenly to the water's surface. It was a fairly routine procedure, but one that always had me on the edge of my seat. On this particular occasion, as we dropped on that final hair-raising manoeuvre, I held my breath and closed my eyes. As we headed toward the wharf, I opened my eyes to behold a wondrous sight. A figure resplendently swathed in a silken gown was standing on the end of the dock, with arms wide open, thrust to the sky. It was Alan! He had bedecked himself out in a peacock-coloured Japanese robe and had come to celebrate my arrival on that death-defying plane. It was an impactful lesson for me!

A few years later, Alan died. News of his passing on to what he believed to be merely a new level of consciousness came in a small envelope sent by his wife. On the card was a simple incomplete circle drawn with a single brushstroke. In typical Alan Watts style, all it said was: *"Listen closely and you will hear the sound of Alan's laughter as it circles the world!"*

I listened. I heard. I *celebrated!* Alan's lesson was completed.

> *We say the only things certain are death and taxes. And the death of each one of us now is as certain as it would be if we were going to die five minutes from now. So where's your anxiety? Where's your hangup? Regard yourself as dead already so that you have nothing to lose. A Turkish proverb says, 'He who sleeps on the floor will not fall out of bed.' So in the same way is the person who regards himself as already dead.*

. . . Alan Watts[13]

Fear of Flying

Flying in aircraft has been similarly terrifying for me. Whenever I was in an aircraft, I never fully put my weight onto the seat, hoping that I could somehow defy gravity, and not provide any extra stimulus for the aircraft to lurch into disaster. I thought I would never overcome my intense anxiety at flying. The very thought of flying through turbulence invited images of mayhem and disaster to overwhelm my mind, and sweat would pour from me.

One day, while Ben and I were flying through gale-force winds over the Pacific, the plane was buffeted about, and shocks shuddered through the cabin as the plane was bounced first this way, then that. With each bump, the aircraft threatened to flip over. I was panicked and terrorized, and images of being splattered on the ground, pitched from 30,000 feet, filled my crazed mind. Wildly I braced myself through each shock, my whole body quivering with terror. In the midst of the horror, I was floating wild-eyed near the roof of the plane. And then, a calm quiet voice floated up from a long ways below: it was Ben, talking to me in a very gentle manner. Although Ben was actually in the seat next to me, it seemed that his voice was coming from somewhere very far away, down below me. The calm steady familiar tone of my friend's voice reached into me: "Jock, if we're really going to go down, it won't do us any good for you to be on the ceiling of the aircraft in a panicked state. Come down here, come into your body, and be with me. If we're really going to die, let's spend our last few minutes together, and experience dying together."

I immediately snapped into my body, and felt tremendous relief in being in contact. I felt a quiet calm, realizing that I could choose to be present and to share whatever occurred with my friend. From this recognition, I became aware that I could not control the aircraft. And I could see that there was no sense in worrying about what I couldn't control. What I could control was my *presence* with Ben. With this recognition came a feeling of calm strength, and faith. And the panic subsided, even in the midst of tremendous turbulence.

Flying has never been so terrifying again. Now, when I fly, I recognize that my feelings of anxiety arise as the aircraft bumps; however, I have learned to focus my attention on my feelings for Ben, and the panic retreats into the background. Recently, to my amazement, I have even begun to enjoy the turbulence, sharing this exhilaration with Ben. I have grown in confidence of myself and my loving; I now have a faith that I will be able to face whatever hand fate deals me. And the panic reaction simply does not burst into full force; the precursor feelings still come, but they do not take root and overcome me.

This profound change is burned in my memory and experience. I am no longer the victim of my fear of flying; I can experience my anxiety, and share it, like I share other feelings, without disappearing from contact. I have been cured, through my loving.

Jock

Fear is the mind-killer. Fear is the little death that brings total obliteration. I will face my fear. I will permit it to pass over me and through me. And when it has gone past me I will turn to see fear's path. Where the fear has gone there will be nothing. Only I will remain.

. . . F. Herbert[14]

Letting Go

I have always had difficulty in letting go of those I love. Sometimes I explain this as being a consequence of my own insecurity, or my lifelong sense of loneliness, or by the fact that I am a typical astrological Cancerian who innately will hold on. Whatever the reasons, I generally tend to feel much emotional pain when those close to me have to leave.

During my early years of group leading, I was especially sensitive to this issue. After working with the most intimate details of people's lives, I would feel a close bond with all of the participants; they would feel the same with one another as well as with me. At the end of each group, we all would suffer much sadness.

I came to hate the last day of every group! Awakening at dawn on such a day, I began my typical obsessing about having to say goodbyes. I berated myself for having chosen to work in such a way, repeatedly having to confront my dread of endings after so much shared closeness. I wondered about the advantages of doing my work in more of a traditional manner of emotional distance; but I quickly rejected that line of defensive thought.

As the sun rose that morning, throwing light upon my gloom, I was suddenly struck by an enlightening awareness. The sun heralded a new day, full of new possibilities. In like manner, the disbanding of the group marked the return of all of its members to lives in which they were about to embark upon new abilities to face their old situations.

Rather than that day being full of endings, I realized that it was the dawn of *new beginnings!* Best of all, I had enjoyed the privilege of being with so many people interested in gaining information and tools to embark upon their journeys in life in new ways.

My heart was flooded with joy as I began to live life *not* from ending to ending, but rather, *from new beginning to new beginning!*

The Fourth Dimension

I have had many friends who seem to possess unusual psychic powers. One of my first experiences was with David Young, who informed me of my "spirit guide" whom he described as a big, black, powerful African man named "Tuwaea." I received that information with some amusing skepticism and filed it in my mind in a "useless information" drawer along with Jack Schwartz's observations about my "golden ray." Over the years, although filled with doubts, I have been drawn to people who appear to be so gifted, seeking from them whatever information they could or would divulge. Such a compulsion has led me at various times to study such fields as astrology, the tarot, spiritism, exorcism and many other aspects of the occult, now referred to as "Psi phenomena."

Although to this day I remain a skeptic, I have had some unusual experiences that have caused me to doubt my skepticism. After I met David, friends arranged for me to meet a "psychic" named Clem, who lived on our Gulf island. Entering the room where I was to be introduced to her, I saw the back of this sweet, diminutive, elderly lady, sitting in a chair facing away from me. She turned to greet me, and upon seeing me, reacted with a visible start. As I shook her hand, I asked her for the cause of her startled reaction. She replied, "I was struck by your spirit guide who accompanied you into the room—he is so black, so big, so powerful!" I was thunderstruck! The description was exactly the same as provided by David Young. With a tremulous voice, I asked if she by any chance could determine my guide's name. After a few moments of deliberation, she said, "His name is Tuwaea." My doubts began to crumble.

During one workshop with David Young, we participants requested a midnight sitting of a "psychic circle." My interest in such an occurrence was somewhat stimulated by an underlying desire to lampoon what I believed to be mystical nonsense. At the stroke of midnight, a dozen of us brave souls gathered to create our experiment. Although we had turned the heat on in the room, it remained unusually chilly, which I thought to myself seemed overly dramatic. David turned out the lights, requesting that we sit in silence and speak only to describe unusual phenomena. Minutes ticked by very slowly; the silence was broken only by the shifting of bodies and a few nervous giggles and coughs.

In the pitch darkness, I slowly became aware of heavy breathing behind my right shoulder. It was so exaggerated that I was certain that somebody was attempting to play an absurd trick on me. I was too indignant to be frightened. I shouted into the dark room, "Whoever is doing that, cut it out! You're not funny!"

From somewhere in the darkness, David's English-accented voice rolled out: "What's the trouble, Ben?"

"Some jerk is trying to frighten me by breathing heavily behind me!" I complained.

"Whoever it is, please stop," David said with a much more accepting tone than my own.

This scene was played out several times, always beginning with the heavy breathing. With each successive time, I became increasingly annoyed and whiny. I was in the middle of shouting out another such protest when the lights suddenly came on! David had gone to the light switch, and upon hearing my protest, he immediately turned the light on—initially I thought he did so as a way of punishing my tormentor. Upon reflection, I believe he wanted to prove to me that there was nobody substantial there behind my back. Whatever his reason, I discovered that nobody in the flesh was responsible for the breathing. The hairs on the back of my neck rose in fright. My mind went into tilt: if no-*body*, what then?

I did not get my answer that night. As a matter of fact, all I derived in that experiment was an assortment of weird happenings, such as some force pulling one of our members out of the circle! I was filled with unanswered questions.

Later that same week, my friend Jock, asleep in his own room, was awakened by the sensation of some eerie visitation. Coming out of a deep sleep, he thought he imaged the figure of a past friend who had died in an accident. Frightened, he ran to David's room to shake him awake. "David! David! Wake up!" he exclaimed. "There's a *spirit* in my room!" Being only slightly annoyed at being so rudely awakened, David groggily replied, "Of course. They're *everywhere!* Go back to sleep."

Possession

After knowing my psychic friend Clem for awhile, I began to understand some psychic phenomena through her eyes. She liked having me around when she would sit in a healing circle because she claimed that I was a passive "medium." To satisfy my constant questions, she attempted to explain how my "light" could be seen in the "other" dimension. "Lost" souls who have not yet found their way to the "other side" for a variety of reasons (such as sudden death, or suicide) would be tempted to follow such lights as mine as a beacon to "pass through" to their final resting place. In other words, they would "possess" some body, hopefully only momentarily as a means of salvation. If things go wrong, some spirits decide to stay in that body rather than moving on; such were Clem's beliefs. Her life's work was to help such lost souls through what she referred to as a "healing circle." Through repeated experience, I began to feel some confidence at accompanying Clem in her work, even though I never lost my scientific skepticism.

My big test arrived when Clem requested that Jock and I assist her in a healing circle for a young man whose brother had committed suicide many years ago. Preceding that event, this man had been diagnosed as suffering from a schizophrenic process; since his brother's death, he had seemed to put his life "on hold." Clem held the belief that the dead brother was possessing this young man because he had not "crossed over" due to his premature death related to his suicide. Even though that idea seemed totally absurd to us, we agreed to participate for reasons of both curiosity and caring.

On the eventful day, we assembled in a circle in a comfortable living room. After Clem had administered her usual rites that would ensure our protection, she touched the young man with both hands, her eyes closed while she murmured some repetitive undecipherable incantations. I gave up trying to hear or understand. She then had me put my hands on the man's shoulders, and to my knowledge, nothing seemed to happen. Yet, after five such minutes, we parted from one another to return to our places in the circle. In the ensuing conversation, the young man said that he felt better, which I had a hard time believing. Yet, I stayed present with my skepticism.

Suddenly, the unexpected happened! Clem abruptly rose to her feet, her head extended, her eyes fixated upward, and her body began to slowly sway. This sudden turn of events was a shock to us all. We heard Clem ask rhetorically, "What's happening?" Some disembodied voice came through her, "I was hung and can't find my way."

Everything was happening too quickly for me to defend myself with either my rationality or skepticism! Suddenly, I experienced myself being *displaced* or some such feeling. It was as though somewhere inside of myself I was pushed aside, and I was no longer in charge of me. I have no idea of the time that I spent in that condition—it seemed like an eternity, although my colleagues report that it was only a few moments. The next thing I was aware of was a rising and emerging soul-curdling scream that originated somewhere in indescribable depths within me, then passed through my throat and mouth. I could not *feel* fear; I *was* all fear! I remember thinking that I was lost forever, and I would have panicked if I were capable of doing so. Then my consciousness was blank.

The next thing I was aware of was Jock leaping across the room to hold me tightly in his arms, calling my name over and over again. He told me later that he was alarmed to see me turn a horrible colour and to hear me emit a strangled scream (that I had experienced as being an ear-shattering one). Worst of all, because we had so practiced remaining constantly present with one another, he had suddenly experienced me disappearing from his purview. In shock, he had flown across the room to recover me; and recover me he did!

Later, as my world returned to order, Clem explained that I had been used as a conduit for a man's soul! She had been able to read that this man had been a criminal who had been hanged, but had not found his way to the "other side." During our healing circle, he had spotted my "light" and had followed it to "pass through and on." I was too confused to question her any further about the event. I was just glad that it was over and swore that I would not repeat it if I could help it.

Unfortunately, over the next few days, I felt very vulnerable—as though I might easily again be displaced by some force outside of myself. The vulnerability would increase and diminish in waves, gradually lessening in intensity with time. I found solace and security by remaining close to Jock who had clothed himself in an armoured stance to protect himself as well as me. I was reassured.

Since that time, I have been very careful about investigating anything else that remotely resembles the occult, even though my curiosity seems constantly pulled in that direction.

Capitulation

For a short time, Jock and I were reckless about investigating the occult. Among some psychic circles, rumour had it that we were especially good at exorcisms. One time, because of that reputation, we were asked to visit some people in Seattle who were certain that their house was haunted. Again, our curiosity won out and we accepted the invitation.

Upon entering that house (which was old but well cared for), we were somewhat uneasy about what we were planning to undertake. The residents described seeing shadowy figures and experiencing chilling feelings in various parts of their home; they lived in constant fear, never knowing what next they might stumble upon. They all believed that some evil force was occupying the house, and they wanted to be rid of it.

Proceeding with what we had learned from our mentors, we decided to try to communicate with these "spirits" through the use of a tapping table. Upon our request, our hosts supplied us with a small, light, wooden table around which we gathered. Placing our hands on the surface, with our fingertips touching, we began to speak to the ethers, requesting whatever spirits that were present to talk with us by rocking the table so that its feet would tap out the alphabet to spell messages to us.

Initially, the table moved as requested, but we could make no sense of the tapped-out alphabet. No words were decipherable; the tapping was erratic, and we gradually were becoming annoyed and frustrated. Suddenly, it occurred to us that whoever we were talking with was either being capricious or couldn't spell! We had the sudden inspiration to ask how old the spirit was, and it tapped out five years! No wonder we couldn't decipher any words! We asked if there were any grown-up spirits around, and upon being answered in the affirmative, we requested their presence.

Suddenly, the table moved with a firmness that was rather intimidating. Now, the spelling was perfect, but the feeling was definitely threatening. Whoever we were in communication with was obviously bad-tempered and upset with something. The more we asked, the worse the responses became. The table began to tap out the answers with loud thuds as the table rocked with great impetus. Try as we would, we could not get answers to our timid inquiries as to the reasons for the anger that filled the house. In one final act of defiance, while responding to one of our questions, the table literally rose into the air (with our fingers still on the top) and smashed down on the floor, breaking into pieces as it landed! Discretion (or cowardice) being the better part of valour, we scooped up our belongings, apologized for being unable to be of any help, and beat a hasty retreat away from the toxic atmosphere of that house.

Our advice to our hosts—MOVE!

Explaining the Inexplicable

My two sons met my psychic friend, Clem, while they were pre-teens. Needless to say, they were fascinated with her psychic abilities and would ask me countless questions about how anyone could tell the future. I struggled to find a metaphor that they might understand, ultimately arriving at the following one.

I said that in our everyday thinking that depends on our five senses, we are time-bound. We visualize that the clouds rain down on us, the water collecting into streams that form rivers that run into the sea. There, evaporation takes place, forming clouds that then rain down upon us to repeat the cycle. Usually, as we think about these events, one follows the other *in time*. When we are located at point B, the events that occurred at point A are described as having taken place *in the past*; the events that will take place at point C are thought of as *the future*. My sons nodded their heads to denote their understanding.

I continued. Suppose that there is no such thing as time. Suppose that at this very moment, the clouds are raining down, the streams are being rivers that are part of oceans that are evaporating into clouds. In other words, suppose that there is no past, present or future—everything would be happening *now!* If this were the case, at this very instant, we could see the past, something that the boys could readily conceive of (although their belief was that it was because of their previous experience). If we were not bound by time—if somehow we could escape from whatever binds our minds to time, at this very instant, we would be able to see the entire picture. There would be no past, no present, no future. It would all just *be!*

At this junction, my sons were perplexed, but still with me. I continued.

Suppose that some people like Clem, who are said to be psychic, for some unknown reason could slide in or out of the time restriction. They then would be able to have a glimpse of the whole picture, or perhaps selected parts of that landscape. The parts that are *ahead* of where we are currently observing would be described as the *future*; the parts *behind* would be the *past*. Although it made no *logical* sense to my mind-time-bound sons, they were astonished to be able to say that they *understood!*

"Then, could anyone be able to do that?" they asked. I replied that I didn't know; however, in my experience I have found that through practice, many who never believed they could were able to develop such skills. I have even wondered what would happen to those who suddenly spontaneously experience such things without either intention or practice. Surely they might become confused or even frightened. Perhaps this may be a factor in some mental illnesses?

The ramifications of such ideas became too complicated and perhaps too absurd to pursue any further with my boys. However, oftentimes when I am alone with my musings, these pictures float back into my consciousness and I continue to wonder. . . .

Hero

I am not a skier. For some still inexplicable reason, when my sons were born, I conjectured that some day in the future, they would like to ski. Hence, I bought a condominium in the newly developing Whistler ski resort. At the time of the purchase, the units were just being completed. Excited, a friend and I drove up from Vancouver with a load of furniture.

Upon arrival early on a crisp winter evening, I was shocked by the amount of cleaning that was required before I could move in. Without even eating dinner, we set about the task of scrubbing and dusting before moving in the furniture up the high stairs. We toiled and sweated late into the evening, finally reaching a point of organization in which we could comfortably clean our own selves up and possibly scrape up some little morsel of food. It was now 1:00 a.m.

Throwing our weary bodies upon the newly positioned furniture for a breather, we happened to notice a glow of dancing warm light on the snow outside of the condo. Passing through the living room's sliding glass door onto the high deck, we leaned against the rail to search for the source of the light. To our horror, we saw flames beneath our unit, licking up to the floor, which was built on stilts. It was as though we were sitting on the surface of a stove—and we were about to be fried!

Panic-stricken, my friend and I leapt into action. Because the flames already were so high beneath us, we knew that we had little time. All the furniture that we had so carefully placed in the newly cleaned rooms had to be quickly re-moved. Lugging them down the stairs was out of the question, so we proceeded to throw everything over the balcony railing to the snow banks some twenty feet below. Soon, the heat became too much for us, so we joined the growing crowd of people. As the entire complex was so new, nobody knew the existence or locations of firefighting equipment. We heard that volunteer firefighters from a nearby village were on their way. Clambering down the hill, we ourselves had discovered a fire hydrant fairly close to our unit, but of course we had to wait for the hose to arrive with the volunteer firemen.

While our condominium was being eaten up by flames, I climbed up and down that hill many times, checking first for the location of the hydrant, then for the arrival of the firefighters. When they arrived, I helped distribute water hose all through the condo complex, again running up and down that infernal hill! About then, we discovered to our amazement that the hose coupling was the wrong size! We needed an adapter. For some reason, I was given the task of running down the road to the nearest telephone to request such a thing from the contact people in the town. By this time, I had run further and had climbed more hills than I had ever done in such a short period of time.

The flames had now spread throughout the complex (later investigation revealed a faulty installation of heating elements around the water pipes), and we had not as yet established an effective water system. Up and down I ran to inform the firefighters that the adapter was on its way. I was exhausted. Yet another trip down the hill was necessary to pick up the arriving adapter, so down I clambered another time. Upon the return climb, my resources suddenly became completely depleted. I fell face down into the snow drift, panting heavily for air, but unable to take one more step.

At that critical moment, some new onlooker began to pass me. I feebly cried out to him. As he approached me, he must have been startled to see me weakly lift my arm into the air, offering up to the heavens in his direction the essential adapter. "Take this to the top," I rasped in my heavy breathing. "They need it to fight the fire! I can't make it to the summit." At that moment, I had the vision of myself as hero, passing on the torch as I lay exhausted, uttering something like, "Be it yours to hold it high!" Accompanied by an imagined movie fanfare, the tableau in my mind almost moved me to tears; I sank back into the snow bank, feeling that I had given my all.

Unfortunately, my heroism went by unnoticed. I was a hero only in my own eyes. I since have learned that that is enough!

Skiing

Once I had bought my condominium at the ski resort at Whistler in anticipation of wholesome weekends with my two sons (who were little more than babies at that time), I set about the task of learning how to ski. Dave, a good friend who was a ski enthusiast, agreed to teach me. He helped me to get outfitted and ultimately packed me up to head for the mountain slopes. On the children's bunny hill, I managed to stand somewhat erect for awhile, scooting around the little children who (unlike my good self) seemed to be having a lot of fun.

After a few hours of my fumbling around, Dave, who lived with the belief that a person should always push his edge, convinced me to come up a short T-bar lift with him. There, on the brow of a small hill, I felt like I was on top of Kilimanjaro. Dave spent a good amount of time attempting to reassure me, but I was loath to give the slope a try. Mentally, I was closely enumerating all the hazards of letting myself sail downhill, when whatever confidence I had was shattered as I witnessed another inexperienced novice recklessly plummet down to the bottom where he ran smack into a small tree! His ski tracks stopped abruptly on either side of the trunk, reminding me of many cartoons of a similar nature that I had seen in my youth. Needless to say, it required every ounce of Dave's powers of persuasion to finally get me to the bottom. Not only that, but in direct opposition to any shred of my common sense, I repeated the ordeal several times, being assured that each time I succeeded would make the next easier and more enjoyable. I experienced neither.

The next day, Dave said that I could probably try out the next level by coming up the lowest ski lift with him; if I chose not to ski down, he said that I would be able to return via the lift. That sounded reasonable enough to me, so with Dave by my side, I found myself in the chairlift, thrilling about becoming one of the "big" people who could ski. But all of a sudden, disaster loomed! As we approached the disembarking site, Dave happened to casually mention that I was going to have to ski down a slight incline as I got off. Omigawd! I could have killed Dave there and then—surely any court of criminal law would understand my need for violent revenge for having been duped! Is that not justifiable homicide? All he could say was, "I guess I forgot to tell you." No apologies, no sympathy for my ultimate destruction!

It must have been amateur day on the slope. As we arrived at the disembarking area, I was befuddled by the confusion and activity all around me as people were skiing down the small slope, some falling while others piled up behind them. I became one of that pile, completely lacking any skills to successfully manoeuvre around the melee. Once I was disentangled, I looked around at the view that Dave thought would make my trip worthwhile. It was unsuccessful. All I could see were obstacles to my health and well-being. In a mangy mood, I removed my skis and took the lift back down.

Over the next few years, I persisted in what ended up to be relatively unsuccessful attempts to accustom myself to this unrewarding sport. Another good friend who was an expert in motivational and sports psychology became excited by the challenge of teaching me and my wife how to ski. Accompanying us onto the bunny slopes, he gave us a standard rap of proper mental attitudes and some basic (easy!) instructions, then left us to practice as he enjoyed a quick run down the slopes. We slipped around for a while before managing a most unbelievable achievement. Accidentally coming toward one another from different angles, we collided and clung to one another with our skis crossed one on top of the other! As we stood helplessly trapped in this position, our expert friend came sailing down the slopes. In utter amazement, he exclaimed that this had never happened to him; he was totally unaccustomed to failure in his teachings. I could not tell him of the slight swelling of pride within my chest, knowing that I had been a first.

Over the ensuing years, my family showed little interest in the sport. For a few years, I continued to bungle around on skis, believing that one day I would get it and suddenly come flying down from the heights. It never happened. As a matter of fact, one day while picking myself up from a horrendous fall and shaking myself free from a covering of snow, I got an image of my body splayed against a mountain cliff. It was enough to send a chill up my already frozen being! Having somewhat of a belief in signs sent from the heavens, I took this as a message to give up this unrewarding task.

I have not skied since. Instead, the experience has given me fuel to consider why people are motivated to flirt with death.

A Cure for Height Phobia

I have been afraid of heights for as long as I can remember. This has led to many humorous stories as we climb high buildings on our world travels. I never like to admit defeat; so, inevitably, I am the one to suggest that we mount any vertical obstacle that our travels provide. As we would climb yet another high structure, Ben would casually lean over the edge, and peruse the bird's-eye view. I would drop to my knees in mock prayer and terror three feet from the railing; then I would edge slowly toward the balcony rail, being careful not to lean, and with a safety grasp on a piece of the building behind. If anyone else came near, or if a wind came up, I would lurch back from the edge. We were used to this phenomenon at various open air height structures.

In Giotto's Tower in Florence, we walked up many flights of stairs that would break out into open areas providing views in all directions at every level. The views were protected by wire mesh that was over twelve feet high; the mesh was about four inches in diameter. I held back from the wire, swooning dizzily. Ben said, "There's no chance that you can fall; the wire mesh will keep you in." I replied, "That's nothing. I can get over that in a flash. I even think I can get through the mesh itself!" In short, I knew that something was compelling me to break free into the open air around the structure.

I was afraid to step on the open grates that showed through to the floors below. Even though countless climbers had undoubtedly stepped on it before, I just knew that I was going to represent the ultimate stress that would cause the grates to cave in, plunging me through all the floors of the structure to my certain death. And I could see it all before me.

When we reached the top of Giotto's Tower, it was by now late afternoon, and the light was falling in the sky. We went out onto the tiniest balcony I had ever witnessed. It seemed to me that the width was no greater than a two-by-four, and the railings seemed to only come up to my knees. Ben casually leaned over the railing, and chattily commented on the marvellous view. I lurched backwards, and crouched into a protective stance, to shield myself from the wind that was rising. I could see myself being flung into the sky by a sudden gust, and hurtling toward the ground all in an instant. My life flashed before my eyes again. I tolerated the scene for as long as I could, and then turned to casually stride inside to safety, only to find the door to the interior locked!

In horror, I saw myself huddled on that little ledge through the night, waiting for the gust of God's wind to take me home to my maker. I wept piteously; Ben had no sympathy, and strolled around as if all was well. I crawled around the ledge, trying to make small talk as my brain screamed, "I'm going to die!" And the thought came, "Why don't I just jump and get it over with? That's what I'm eventually going to do anyway, to end this agony."

And in a flash I saw it. I was always afraid of high places because I could see myself flying through the air, jumping from the place. Indeed, it was not so much someone else, or some external force that I feared. It was my infernal imagination, which sent me hurtling through the air each time. I could imagine it; and if I wasn't continually vigilant, I might succumb to the pull, and just leap over. For, indeed, I had repeated visions of leaping. *It wasn't the height. It was myself that I feared. I knew what I was capable of.*

This even happened at the World Trade Center in New York, where the entire view is through floor-to-ceiling glass. My on-my-knees approach to the view was somewhat reminiscent of the pilgrims at the Shrine at Guadalupe, where worshippers shuffled on their knees toward their destination. I knew that I must not put myself physically in the position in which some cosmic or preternatural event might strike—I must not tempt fate. So, my imagination of disaster included not only my subterranean impulses, but the wrath of deities and cosmic forces; I was being singled out by God and the universe for especially harsh dealings. I was a modern Job! Such arrogance to think I was so important. Anyway, I forced myself up to the window, and even tentatively touched the glass with a little pressure, to see if I could stand being so near. And I managed to do it without fainting, or the glass giving way. I felt triumphant but somewhat weak-kneed as we went back down the elevator after this odyssey.

After I had calmed down from the World Trade Center incident, I curiously asked Ben, "How is it that you are not afraid to lean over and look out with the glass at your forehead? Aren't you afraid that the glass will give way, and you'll go plummeting?" Ben's reply appealed to the scientist in me: "It's a matter of logic; someone has carefully designed these windows to be safe, and thousands of people have been here; statistically, the chances of my being the one to break the safe sequence is infinitesimally small. So, I don't see that being afraid or panicked stands to reason. It's just not worth the bother to worry about it." And Ben's loving laughter and ridicule helped to put the situation into perspective for me. Subsequent to that, I found that I could venture closer to the edges of high places, with the logic that the chances of falling were very slim indeed. (Of course, I had already acknowledged that the greatest danger came from within myself—that I was afraid, not of falling or being pushed, but of jumping! I could visualize myself going over the edge, and in this image, I recognized that in a way, for excitement, *I wanted to jump!*)

And so, by this process of talking and sharing, rather than keeping the insanity of these obsessions to myself, I have managed to climb many high structures, and scare myself out of my wits. And I have still survived! And over time, my fear has lessened. I am accumulating experience that I do not jump, and that engineers generally do make safe structures. By the time Ben and I and our three sons had our father-son bonding trip up the Empire State Building some years ago, the boys were surprised to find that the test they made—leaning with full body weight against the observation tower glass—could easily be passed by me. I am now one of the intrepid men of the sky!

Jock

Vulnerability

When I first began to lecture, I would work slavishly over the text that I was to present. I wanted to create a good impression, to make the audience believe that I was intelligent, believable and competent. This motivated me to organize, plan and memorize—an immense task full of pitfalls and anxiety. I was fearful of the possible non-acceptance of my listeners who might see me falter, make a mistake, or lose control. All of this changed during one of my lectures.

I was the keynote speaker at a large convention of teachers, an audience in the thousands in a large auditorium. I was talking about educating and dealing with children. While speaking about some of the youngsters that I was seeing, I began to become emotional over their plights, their struggles, and their pain. At first, my need to be seen as manly and in control was strong enough to keep me on target, with only a slight tremor in my voice. However, the more I remembered, the more compassion I began to experience. Finally, my voice cracked completely and tears welled up in my eyes. To my horror, I was rendered speechless! I stared into the faces of my audience in mute helplessness. The total silence that filled the huge auditorium seemed unbearable as I expected the worst—humiliation, rejection, scorn?

To my astonishment, the entire body of people rose to their feet in silent respect. In many of their eyes I could see that they too had tears. Then, the hall filled with their applause as we all began to weep uncontrollably. Ever since then, I have no longer feared being vulnerable before audiences, and I have reduced planning to a minimum. I have learned that in teaching, what is most appreciated is the sharing of my self, not my information.

Vulnerability is a symptom of *strength*, not weakness.

Genes and Memes

As investigators of human behaviour, Jock and I have always had to consider the inherited effects of genetics and the learned patterns of interaction in the family and society. Over the years, our opinions have shifted in our judgments as to the relative importance of each of them.

An example of this problem is the characteristic of Jock's narcissism. When I first laid eyes on Jock, the newly graduated hot-shot physician, I was amazed at the obvious degree of narcissism I found in his social presentation. While shaking his hand, I began to laugh, saying "You've got to be kidding!" Over the ensuing years, we both devoted much attention to investigating the source of his self-absorption. Finding little evidence of this characteristic in his family led us to believe that most of it must be an idiosyncratic defence developed to handle his low self-esteem.

Our attitude changed with our experience of Jock's son Justin, who was only a year old when his parents separated. Until he was five years old, Justin and his mother travelled to distant places, resulting in no contact between father and son for much of Justin's formative years. The opportunity for learned behaviour associated with Jock was severely limited. Upon Justin's eventual return into our lives, we were struck by the remarkable similarities of his behaviour to Jock's.

For as long as I have known Jock, I have noticed his love affair with the mirror. He often glances into one, sometimes peering intensely and self-critically. I have observed his individually characteristic way of cocking his head, with neck thrust forward, eyes peering intently, eyebrows furrowed, lips slightly pursed, while fondling and combing a stray strand of hair. As this is behaviour that Jock only displays in the privacy of his own room, it would have been impossible for Justin to have been able to mimic him. However, when he first came to visit us after such a long absence, I was struck by seeing him peer into a mirror *in exactly the same way* as his father!

Up until this time, we had believed in the genetic transmission of *physical* characteristics from generation to generation; we thought that *behavioural* characteristics were learned or copied. With our intimate experience of our sons, we have become increasingly impressed by their behaviours that so closely resemble ours; not all of these similarities can easily be attributed to learned behaviour. Is it possible that they, too, can be genetically transmitted? What helped us out of this theoretical dilemma was the discovery of a concept of behavioural patterns called *memes*; could these be possibly passed on in a manner similar to genes? In the fields of family therapy and twin studies, a growing body of evidence is suggesting that this is so. It is interesting to witness such evidence in our own progeny.

It is sobering to realize that, no matter how hard we strive to make life easier for our children, they are going to have to face the same problems (and be blessed with the same positive attributes) as ourselves. The influence of our genes and memes is strong; our consciousness, continued vigilance, and resolve must be stronger if we hope to help our progeny to overcome any undesirable family traits.

It is said that the dancer Isadora Duncan wrote to (G.B.) Shaw that good eugenics indicated they should have a child together. "Think of it! With my body and your brains, what a wonder it would be," she said. Shaw replied, "Yes, but what if it had my body and your brains?"

. . . C. Fadiman[15]

Father-Son Talks

With our sons, Ben and I did not agree with the school of punishment. We wanted our children to become sensitive to others and to be responsible for themselves and their actions. We believed that punishment only served to keep youngsters from learning from their actions. When children were punished, they would be judged as "bad," and would then be given a sentence that fit the crime. We believed that in this method the children would only come to judge themselves harshly, without having any real awareness about themselves.

Instead, we wanted our boys to be responsible for their actions and attitudes, and to meet the consequences for whatever they had done. And so, we discussed consequences ahead of time, and then made sure that we made the consequences stick. For example, if the boys did not eat what was on their plate, the consequence would be that they would not get any more food that evening—and that included no dessert! The consequence of not eating everything they had taken was that they could not have more food, including the prize of dessert. The boys learned to take on their plate only what they were prepared to eat. They were not bad if they didn't eat all their plate; they simply did not get more. There was no blame; there were only actions and consequences . . . and learning.

Whenever one of our boys would not live up to an agreement, we did not punish them. Instead, we sat down and had a conversation, in order to learn about the meaning of the situation. We did not want them to feel bad about themselves; we wanted them to learn about the consequences of their behavior.

My son Justin learned to recognize when a father-son awareness talk was coming. In my endeavour to be fair and not critical, I would struggle to find the exact words to express my feelings without blaming. I apparently would screw up my face and put my hand to my forehead in a hand posture that Justin can mimic to this day. I would soften my voice and, with a strained look on my face, I would say, "Justin, I'd like to talk with you."

He and I both found these discussions very distressing. I felt bad when he would feel ashamed, or hurt, or hard on himself. And yet I persevered, because I did want him to learn to be responsible and to know my feelings. He found the intensity of focus on him and his behaviour at times to be almost intolerable. One day, in frustration, he blurted out, "Why don't you just hit me like other fathers do with their sons? It would be easier than these talks!"

Jock

Teaching Autonomy

Following my divorce from my wife, our two sons lived with her and visited me at regular intervals, which I valued. When my youngest son, Randy, turned sixteen, he became more interested in driving cars and being with his friends than being with his parents. On one visit during my fiftieth birthday, I was to be honoured at a large gathering in Vancouver; so I was sentimentally looking forward to driving to the city with him.

Just before we were to embark upon our trip, Randy informed me that he was planning to drive to town with a friend of his who had just received his driver's license. With hurt feelings and injured pride, I flew into a rage, reminding him of how little time we had together, and how special this event was to me. In my worst display of paternalism, I questioned his appreciation of all that I had sacrificed for him. In the face of my anger, he appeared frightened and guilty, ultimately declaring that he would accompany me to Vancouver.

I refused to accept his acquiescence. I acknowledged that my anger was a purely selfish thing, arising from my own need rather than his. Having worked with adolescents for so long, I said that I understood and supported his desire to be with his peers. Furthermore, I would not agree to his abandoning his inclinations in order to please me or to assuage my anger; I preferred that he learn how to stand by his decisions, no matter how much pressure is exerted from outside sources and authority—to be master of his own fate.

As for myself, I wanted him to understand that I was capable of handling my own hurt feelings, and that anger was my own infantile attempt to control him. He had no obligation to be responsible for my emotional reactions. In spite of my disclaimers, he continued to be flooded with guilt and still wished to accompany me, which I steadfastly refused.

Ever since that episode, the two of us have had occasion to refer back to that incident; his brother believes that Randy was treated unfairly and not given the chance to change his mind. I have continued to insist that to respect his authentic being, he would have had to change his mind for reasons other than guilt over my hurt feelings. Compassion is one of the alternative motivations. Whatever was true about that encounter, Randy has had much to consider whenever he has found himself in similar situations—is it guilt or compassion?

That has made the experience worthwhile.

Psychological health requires transforming our infantile fears of abandonment and punishment and our inappropriate shame and guilt into a mature set of values. When we violate our chosen values or fail to live up to ideals that we honor, we will feel an appropriate, mature sense of guilt or shame. A healthy adult must take responsibility for creating a conscience that will protect his or her sense of what is important and sacred.

. . . Sam Keen[16]

Little Emperors

I was a very controlling little kid. For example, I would not eat unless I could have five-sixths of the dining room table to drive my trucks on. My parents and my grandmother were huddled down at one end, with elbows tucked in tight, while the Little Emperor was playing trucks with one hand and munching a sandwich with the other. If I didn't get all this space, I would feel hurt. And they didn't want that. So I got my way. Entitled little beast!

From my early experiences in controlling my own family, I have learned a great deal about this game. And so I now know how to deal with little kids who are controlling their parents with their hurt feelings. I am amazed at how early they learn to do this—generally before they can talk.

A common scene in our restaurant in the lodge in the summer involves a young husband and wife and their first-born child, who is still in diapers, not talking, and sitting with them very importantly in one of those little chairs that attach under the side of the table. All goes well until the mother has the audacity to talk to the father, and not lavish total attention on the child. Very soon, the little prince or princess does something to get the attention back: a piece of food or a toy goes on the floor, necessitating the mother's attendance, and an accompanying coo-coo to the child. If the parents go back to their conversation, the child will begin to make more fuss, and soon will make a little squall. If the parents still do not succumb to these control measures, the child will make a full-blown scene.

Because I was this kind of child, I know the game well. I have taken to approaching the table and addressing the child directly. I get my face down close to the contorted visage of the little one, and talk very directly in this fashion: "Shut up, you little monster! Your mother has every right to talk with your father! The entire world does not revolve around your whims! You look dry, and no pins are sticking into you. And you have food and a toy! So, *get a life of your own!*"

To the parents' amazement, this little being, who still does not speak, can understand me very well. Generally the child will stop crying, and will regard me with intense interest. If the little one goes back to the controlling behaviour, I will say, "I mean it. You're in for a miserable life if you don't learn something different!" And generally the child will stop. As I leave, I feel a pair of small eyes boring into my back. For the rest of the family's visit at the resort, the child regards me with solemn intensity. But that child remains in contact with me, and shows a growing respect for me. Often, the child will begin to broaden the basis of contact, and will smile and become more bright with me. Not only will the kid communicate quite directly with me, but also, will play less of the crying game with parents and sibs. By the time the family is ready to leave, the child often has learned more self-occupation.

Jock

From early infancy children are engaged in exploring ways and means of finding their place, of being significant, important. As they discover a technique for reaching this goal, they cling to it, regardless of how many times they are scolded or punished. The unpleasantness of parental reaction does not diminish the satisfaction of feeling important. As long as the method they have chosen brings results, they will stick to it and continue their bid for attention or power.

. . . R. Dreikurs[17]

Meaning What You Say

When my eldest son Kevin entered his adolescence, I began to grow concerned about his tendency toward procrastination. I decided to teach him an object lesson when the opportunity arose, even though I had no idea what form that lesson might take.

One day, I asked Kevin to mow the lawn and he readily agreed. However, days passed without him performing that task; I remained silent. I finally took out the lawn mower and began to cut the grass myself; it was not a big job, and I actually enjoyed the exercise. However, within a few minutes, Kevin rushed out to say that he would take over from me. I declined his offer; he was taken aback.

"Why won't you let me do it?" he asked.

I replied that I had been aware of his promise, but had concluded that he did not mean it when the grass remained uncut for days. He argued that he fully intended to live up to his promise, and that *now* was the time. I answered that *now* was too late—having begun the task, I full intended to complete it.

Feeling disconsolate and guilty, Kevin followed me around the lawn in a vain attempt to change my mind. To this day, he will maintain that I was unfair—that I should have given him the opportunity to fulfill his promise. I continue to disagree, believing that good intentions are not enough.

However each of us has interpreted that event, I notice that my sons now do what they say they will do—in good time!

Whining

Because we did not live with our sons, and only had extended time with them in the summers, we used to go on trips with them to have shared unique experiences and memories. We learned a valuable lesson on one of these "father-son bonding trips."

When Justin was about eight and Randy was about fifteen, Ben and I took them on a tour of California, which included Disneyland, Universal Studios, Sea World, the San Diego Zoo, Beverly Hills, and other highlights of that region. Kevin could not come on that trip; after he heard the reports, he was kind of happy about that.

We were travelling all over Southern California in a tiny rental car, negotiating the perils of the ten-lane freeways, and navigating from one site to the next. To me, it was some kind of odyssey, or even a kind of spiritual quest, to have significant experiences with our sons that would settle into lifelong significant memories. I would sometimes lapse into a reverie about what a wonderful thing this was that we were doing. We were bonding, we were together, we were establishing such intimacy between ourselves.

Then gradually, I noticed that I was becoming quite irritable. I thought at first my discomfiture was the result of the constant tension of driving on the very busy freeways. However, I noticed that my irritation did not subside when we had stopped travelling. I was quite out of sorts; I wondered at the cause. The feeling grew into one of resentment and anger, directed at the boys. I still did not know for sure why I was becoming so angry; I only knew that I was having thoughts of murdering my own son!

Then the awareness suddenly flashed into my mind. After proposing a new destination, which I thought would be replete with fun and adventure, I heard a moaning sound from the back seat where the two boys sat. "Aawuh!" This wasn't a full groan; it was more of a subvocal whimper. But there was a palpable tone of complaint and disagreement in it. I recognized in a flash the source of all my irritation. It was that hideous sound—Aawuh!

"I hate that!" I exclaimed. "Where did you learn to make such a disagreeable sound?" "It works with our mothers," the boys replied.

On questioning, we discovered that the boys would use that little sound—Aawuh—whenever their mothers would ask them to do anything. They found that they could delay doing any task by uttering the whimper. For example, if one of their mothers asked them to cut the lawn, they could utter "Aawuh!" and would find that they would not be expected to do the task for another day or so. They had practiced to make it perfect; and then they had discovered that it was simply fun to do it, and they had begun to use it for the sheer pleasure of letting it roll out of their throats.

We found a democratic solution. Because the boys found so much pleasure in this utterance, we decided that the adults should be able to get in on the fun too. So we banned the expression of "Aawuh!" except at designated times. Every hour, on the hour, we would pull the car over, and we all would let out several "Aawuh!" sounds, with full voice and gusto. We began to laugh together; and we adults began to find the pleasure in shared complaints.

Instead of fighting about it, we found a solution that worked for us all. On returning to Canada, and talking later with the mothers of the boys, we discovered that they had noticed that they too were irritated over that sound. The mothers were most grateful to have the situation clarified.

We always say that anything that is shared can enhance intimacy. We had not realized until this episode that we could have so much father-son bonding by sharing whimpering, moaning and whining. Aawuh!

Jock

Through Parents' Eyes

While working with families, and indeed, within my own family, I have always been amazed at how much influence parental opinions have on children. Certainly, when I was young, it was obvious to me that my parents had much to teach me; it was no problem because I was eager to learn. However, I reached a critical point in my life when I realized the limits of what they had to teach. As I grew to think for myself, my mother especially became increasingly offended by my developing a mind of my own. She frequently would admonish me for wanting to do what I wished to do, rather than what she thought was best for me: "Is that what they're teaching you at school? . . . to not listen to your own parents?" As with most adolescents, I soon stopped letting her know what it was that I was learning.

When I told my parents that I had decided to study psychiatry, they were mortified. In their old Chinese tradition, they believed that messing with another person's mind was akin to some kind of black magic. How could they hold up their heads with pride among their peers if I were to embark upon such a mission? To make matters worse, within a year, my next younger brother, Ernest, embarked upon a similar path.

When we were younger, Ernest and I felt quite close to one another, even though we were dissimilar in many ways. I was a thinker and book reader; he was an artist and creator. We both loved to paint with oils. My own paintings were close replicas of other pictures, while he drew and painted from nature, truly creative in both conception and execution. I would receive praise from my mother for my "pretty" pictures while Ernest would receive a shake of the head and words to the effect of "Why can't you paint nice things like your brother does?" How unfair and unrealistic that must have been for him! He actually was a more creative artist than I.

Through such experiences, I came to understand that the most valuable function of parents is to transmit to their children a *core* system of values that will form the scaffolding upon which all future learning will be hung (I recognize that, in our family, value was placed on industriousness, achievement, honesty, and respect). Neither the parent nor the child should believe that the scaffolding is the building itself. Only the children themselves can construct that.

Ultimately, my own parents somewhat reluctantly arrived at the position of accepting that we children knew more about what we knew, and that they knew more about what they knew. We no longer had to convince one another as to our own points of view. This was when we both began to mature.

> *Maturity comes when you ask not, 'Where have I been wronged?' but instead ask, 'Where can I be fuller?'*
>
> . . . Bennet Wong

A "Sensitive" Child

When we were first working together, Ben would joke with me, poking fun at my shortcomings and foibles. Rather than laugh at his gibes, I would wince and stiffen and be very defensive, essentially killing the fun. I soon came to acknowledge that I was being defensive, and that I did not have much resiliency when it came to taking a joke. Indeed, I also didn't offer humour back. We began to see that I had apparently not developed a sense of humour. When Ben questioned me about this, he said, "Surely there must have been funny events in your past, where you would learn to laugh and enjoy yourself." With a dramatic dour frown, I said that I had not learned to joke because my family had not joked when I was a child. Since I had not been stimulated to laugh, I had not developed the faculty of humour. In effect, I was claiming to be an adult child of parents with no sense of humour!

We accepted this, and I set about the task of overcoming my early developmental arrest by investigating what made humour work. I would watch people make a joke and try to analyze what made the humour go—a serious endeavour indeed! Gradually, I began to see what was happening, and I shyly ventured to make jokes of my own. And I realized that I did have a somewhat rudimentary sense of humour that had apparently arrested at the Grade One level. So poo-poo and bum-bum jokes were a real hit with me!

In the course of this investigation, my parents came out to the west coast to visit. They were laughing and joking with each other, and obviously enjoying life with much humour. Ben said to them, "Wait a minute! You are obviously enjoying a lot of humour. But Jock says that you never joked when he was a child."

"Ah no, not with him," they replied. "It wasn't worth it. When we would joke, Jock would get so upset that the house would be filled with a dark cloud for days. It simply wasn't worth it to joke with him. And so, when we would feel a joke coming on, we would give each other the eye, and go next door to the neighbour's to tell it."

And so, I had won. I was the "sensitive child" who couldn't take a joke, who controlled his whole family with a lack of sense of humour.

Jock

Straight and Tall

During my work with people, I have been impressed by the negative effects of dependency. Both in families and in couples, I began to visualize that individuals who lean upon one another are like trees that grow up beside one another. Trees that depend upon another for support will never grow a strong root system and their trunks become bent and weak; their branches cannot reach out very far, so they can never be in touch with many others. Similarly, people who lean on others remain shallow-rooted and weak, easily falling down in the winds of change; they lack a far reach, so their contacts with others are limited. Oftentimes in life, such weak-rooted people seek relationships with stronger individuals that they can lean upon. If they do so, they abandon the opportunity for themselves to grow straight and tall.

A much happier situation unfolds when two trees (individuals) grow side by side, each developing roots and trunks that will support themselves. Instead of the relief of leaning, the pleasure then is in the interplay of the touching branches and leaves that spread far and wide. Patterns of experience shift and move in the wind, creating ever-changing mosaics of dancing light. Such is the happy situation with autonomous, self-responsible people who are strongly rooted within themselves, yet wish to dance together through life. Each grows straight and tall.

*In today's world, people are more looking for **merging** than what is **emerging** (and what is emerging is the revelation of our relatedness to one another in our separate distinctiveness).*

. . . Bennet Wong

A Scottish Solution

When Ben and I were first in relationship, I was very hesitant to make any long-lasting commitment. I was a true child of the sixties, living for the "here and now" without much concern for the future. I was a pleasant and engaging comrade; however, I now see that I was limiting the scope of my friendships by being so uncommitted. I now recognize that at the bottom of this casual attitude, which I shared at that time with so many others, was my fear of intimacy. I could commit to show up for work on time, and to perform any activity that I wished. Hence, I was a responsible worker and a good professional partner. However, when the work day was done, I was skittish about being tied to any particular pattern of activity. I wanted to be "open" to "whatever happened."

When we moved to Cortes Island, at first we rented a place month-by-month. My Scottish blood was troubled at the poor financial approach; I was aware that purchasing a home was more sensible than continually renting. So, I agreed to purchase a home with Ben, as a business arrangement. I was prepared to commit myself to a mortgage, believing that this was good financial management. My Scottish blood had been calmed; and I still was free within this agreement. I still could come and go as I pleased; I could even rent my portion of the house to someone else if I decided to leave for a time. We lived together in the house, but I was still fervently invested in the freedom of no personal commitments. I gradually acknowledged that life was smoother if I would commit to coming home each night for dinner; I sacrificed some spontaneous whimsy in place of more dependable relating. I was putting my toe in the waters of commitment.

Then I was faced with how long we would be living there. I was there "for the moment." However, an offer came to lead several programs in the coming year; to agree to lead these programs also meant that I was committing to being in that house for a year. The proposition of work was very attractive to me; so I agreed to stay in the house with Ben for a year. And I survived! I had made a commitment, albeit *for a limited period of time.*

We continued in this way for a couple of years, with my insisting on maintaining the freedom of open possibilities for the future beyond our one-year planning. In this way, I kept a foot in the exit door, thus limiting the depth of our friendship and intimacy. I was committed to the relationship *in a limited way,* and beyond the time of one year, I was unfettered. As we discussed this, I became aware that a deep-seated fear of intimacy lurked beneath my insistence on freedom and limited commitments. I began to explore the mental images of being committed for longer periods of time. Each time I did, the prospect brought perspiration to my brow, and my heart raced. I was indeed in panic at the thought of being corralled! I was afraid to commit myself with another person. I was afraid of intimacy.

I determined to overcome this fear. But I found that even if I mouthed the words "I am committed in this relationship," I still had fantasies of being separate and alone. At stressful times in our encounters, these fantasies were strong, and very attractive indeed! I wanted to get over this limitation on my part, but I did not know how!

One day, the solution arrived in the mail, in the form of the renewal form for our *Time* magazine subscription. We had taken only a year's renewal at a time up to that point, in order to keep the freedom of our options open. As I scanned the renewal form, I saw clearly that the longer-term renewal had a decided financial advantage. My Scotsman's fervour for a bargain filled me. With trembling hand, I signed the form for a three-year renewal. As I mailed the envelope, I was overcome with a mixture of satisfaction and enthusiasm for my financial prowess, and gnawing fear that I had surrendered my soul.

As the days progressed, I became used to the idea of being in the same place for three years, in the same relationship. I had expanded my vision of a limited relationship to three years! I had been afraid when my commitment was forever; when it was time limited, I could get my mind and my interest around it, even for an increased period of time.

Since that time, I have not been so afraid of personal commitment. I now readily will fantasize ten or twenty years from now, being with Ben, and having our life together. What saved me from a life of shallow isolation was my Scottish blood, and my fervour for a bargain! What providence to have been born as I was!

Now, in working with couples, I often find that one party is afraid of a lifelong commitment; with this fear the individual maintains an unnecessary shallowness. Many people find that they can commit to a limited period of time. So, when couples are facing such issues, I often advise them to make a contract for one month, and re-evaluate the situation at the end of that time. Many people find that they can gradually extend their tolerance for commitment, and thus their intimacy deepens.

Jock

Loving you means being honest with you,
not necessarily saying or doing what you want.

. . . Bennet Wong & Jock McKeen

Non-presence

Before giving a seminar in a large hotel, Jock and I took the opportunity to relax in the swimming pool. Through the large windows overlooking the pool, we could see the lecture hall in which we were to present our lectures the next day. During our sessions, we spoke to the audience with this pool behind us, a pleasant reminder of the fun we enjoy together in recreation as well as work.

Because we know one another so well and are intimately attuned to one another's energy, we have the confidence of providing seamless presentations without interference from one another. Each of us can pick up where the other leaves a thought, in order to further elucidate a subject or to move on to the next idea. We have happily managed to successfully address whatever issues of competition might interfere with our flow—with only one exception.

Although I enjoy answering questions from the floor during our presentations, Jock has some problem ascertaining just exactly what the questioner is asking. When he teaches his own courses in Oriental medicine, he is confident with his responses; but with general information that we have worked out together, he is sometimes easily unnerved. Audiences seem to pick up on his anxiety; because of this and possibly because of my age (to which wisdom is often ascribed), participants frequently address their questions to me. In this sort of situation, Jock's competitiveness can rise to astounding levels of interference.

At this particular session, many questions were coming my way. Typically, Jock's anxiety rose as he kept mental score, 10 questions for Ben, none for Jock! Just as he reached his breaking point, some woman from the back row stood up to ask him a question. Although it was a relatively minor one, Jock rose to create an answer that would be unprecedented in eloquence and breadth! Although his actions were inhibited by the fact that we were positioned behind a table set with white table cloth and a jug of water, he moved his arms with grace and expansiveness as he expounded on the minuscule subject.

While in full flight, his waving arms struck the jug of ice water, sending it flying into my lap! As I was recovering from the shock of the cold water, it occurred to me that I could rightfully be indignant, annoyed, and even angry. But I felt none of these. Partly it was because the swimming pool behind us reminded me that just a few hours ago, I had enjoyed being wet while I swam.

More important, because Jock and I have been accustomed to clearing up differences as they happened, we had no unfinished baggage stored, no unexpressed resentments waiting for the opportunity to being dumped.

In the moment, Jock was horrified over what he had done. He thought that if he talked fast enough to rivet the audience's attention, they might not notice what he had done. Indeed, they remained silent—no laughter, no gasps, no utterances at all! Perhaps they were stunned over what had just transpired, or maybe they were being too polite to let on that they had noticed. After escalating the pitch and fervour of his presentation for a few seconds, he finally lapsed into silence.

With his emotions showing on his face and in his voice, he said that he had to speak about what had just happened. He knew that they must have noticed that he had knocked the ice water into my lap. He confessed that he had not been present with me; shamefaced, he acknowledged his competitiveness and his excitement over being asked a question. He said that he had made an object of the questioner, using her as a means of displaying his knowledge rather than communicating with her as a person. In so doing, he had made objects of both me and himself.

In his acknowledgement, Jock was very personal; his shame was on display. The audience was thunderstruck over his vulnerability. In many of their eyes, tears welled and overflowed. The ensuing silence was filled with their respect. When they finally spoke, they discussed all aspects of the episode—the objectification that occurs with competition, the use of one another for personal gratification, the lack of my anger because of the uncluttered energy between us, and the conversion of objectifying behaviour into personal experience. Everybody seemed to have something to learn, and learn they did. It proved to be a most enlightening experience for us all.

In the end, people were profuse with their praise over our teaching style. The ultimate compliment came with the final question: "Did you guys set up this situation as a way of demonstration?"

Presence

The first episode that I had working with Ben in a group brought a most valuable learning for me.

Ben had accepted an invitation by the Child Welfare League of America to conduct a workshop at a large conference; he was experimenting with experiential exercises, and thought he could handle a group of forty or so in this unusual learning style. A couple of days before he was due to present, the organizers informed him that they had not closed his workshop, and that several hundred people had signed up. Shocked and alarmed, Ben informed them that he would need to bring an associate in order to take charge of such a demand. The organizers agreed, and he invited me. I was intimidated by the prospect, as I was fresh from my medical internship and had not conducted sessions for large groups, much less experiential learning groups. Ben assured me that all would be well, and that all I had to do was agree to be present with him. Well, this seemed easy to agree to; I had done surgery, and I knew about the discipline of unrelenting focus for hours at a time. So I readily agreed to be present for the talk.

We flew to Minneapolis, and were put up in high style, as featured leaders, in a huge suite. I remember the oriental antique furniture and the huge ceilings. The room was immense, with Ben's bed on one side of the room and mine on the other, separated by what seemed like a distance of a half mile. We bid each other goodnight, and settled in to rest up for our presentation the next morning.

After a period of unconsciousness, I woke up startled in the darkened room to the sound of an angry voice calling me. As I rubbed my eyes to open, I saw Ben's figure looming over me, remonstrating with me to wake up. "You promised to stay present, and you went away!"

At first defensive, I retorted, "Of course I wasn't present! I was asleep!" Ben persisted. "What was happening?" he asked. I searched my immediate recall, and noted that I had been dreaming, about a situation that did not include Ben.

I had not considered that he had expected me to be present *in sleep*! Somewhat humbled, I realized there was a lot more to this presence business than I had thought.

I have since found that we can do this—be present with each other—in sleep, or when we are physically separated. Many mothers who have heard this story have nodded knowingly; they knew that they could sleep, and yet wake up immediately if their children in distant rooms were in distress. They knew about being present in sleep, and at a distance.

We have practiced this, and learned that our relationship goes on twenty-four hours a day, even when we are sleeping, or physically separated.

The first opening came in seeing that it could be done.

Jock

 Imagination is more important than knowledge.

. . . Albert Einstein[18]

Learning Non-presence

As a young boy, I was timid, shy, and emotionally isolated. However, I had a deep yearning to join and to belong, so I devoted much of my energy and time trying to figure out how to accomplish those ends. I now believe that it was because of this that I became an avid observer of the human condition. Also, having experienced considerable feelings of rejection, I developed a basic paranoid stance that I have managed to transform into skills of surveillance that have been valuable to me in my chosen profession. Coming from this place of paranoia and isolation had the peculiarly paradoxical effect of necessitating the development of a high degree of *presence*. As a matter of fact, I have become aware that I rarely was able to relax into non-presence either in situations of work or leisure; I have always been poised for action.

This situation was highlighted early in my relationship with my partner, Jock. After working and living with him for several years, I began to notice some telling things about him. Most remarkable was his ability to distance himself from experience (or was it his incapability to stay close in difficult situations?). We would have an argument of some sort. To my astonishment and irritation, he would be able to back away from it without any outward sign of discomfort, while I would fume and pace. He could read or work at his income tax while I was unable to rest or sleep, replaying the incident over and over again in my mind. I often would ask him how he could remain so cool; but as it was a habit developed early in his childhood, he was unable to give me any useful information. Rather, he would puzzle over how I never seemed to be able to let things easily go.

The further we explored our differences, the more obvious it became that Jock was accustomed to remaining *distant* and *non-present* in face of either conflict or situations of intimacy. I had no such skill, being accustomed as I was to always remaining present in order to be ready for any eventual necessary action! Without any guidelines, I began to practice *not caring* when confronted with disagreements. Finally, during one such historical episode, I found myself comfortably and pleasantly unmoved by the situation. Both Jock and I were struck by the difference in me. Like Jock would previously do, I found myself able to read, do mathematical computations, and generally get on with life. Such a relief!

Unfortunately for Jock, my change in attitude came as a shock to his balanced emotional system. He became aware that all of his life had been governed by the *control* he had over his feelings. While others raged, he had remained *cool* and *distant*—essentially *not present*. Now that the tables were turned, he felt at a loss as to how to relate to me; never before had he witnessed my own non-presence. As the day progressed and I remained remarkably cool, he became increasingly anxious. When he informed me of his inner turmoil, I related how puzzling that now seemed to me, as the position of non-presence seemed very comfortable indeed! I even said, "Now I know why you would always retreat to this most comfortable of spaces!"

That night, I had a wonderful sleep; Jock did not. The next morning, he closely studied my face as he asked me how I was. I replied that nothing seemed to have changed—I was as distant and remote as the day before. However, I was no longer enjoying the absence of feelings. I wanted to return to my previous state of presence, even with its possible accompanying discomfort. But both Jock and I were ignorant as to how to effect such a return to the senses. Now I, too, began to worry. As the day progressed, I kept returning to explore my dilemma with Jock, whose brow was becoming increasingly furrowed with concern.

Then it happened! I was looking deeply into Jock's eyes, examining his anxiety, when I noticed them fill with tears—I could feel his pain! At that moment, my feelings of empathy for him returned in a flood of my own tears, and we rejoiced in my return of presence.

Presence, which served my paranoia for so long, now also served my desire to join, to share, and to care.

Never Get Discouraged

For years, Ben and I have been taking out our aggression in daily games of multiple solitaire. One day, in his inimitable fashion, Ben asked, "Why is it that I win most of the games?" Somewhat defensively, I replied, "You don't win *most* of the games. I'll grant that you win *more* than I do, but you don't win most!" At the time, that seemed eminently logical as a retort. Well, to prove our respective theses, we embarked upon keeping score of every game. To my horror, I watched as Ben's score progressively mounted. We would jockey back and forth, with my winning a game here and there; however, he was indeed winning more than I was! I still wasn't prepared to admit that he was winning *most* of the games (pride has its strange contingencies). However, the tabulated evidence proved that I was in trouble. When I finally realized that I was irretrievably down for the count, I wanted a way through with dignity. Realizing that the Vancouver Canucks had just had a bad year, I decided that I could surrender this series, without going back on my original claim. I could declare a loss *for this series* and then begin to count again—just like a new season for other sports.

And so, we began to play again, in a new series. Unfortunately, the story was inevitably the same. I was in the bottom of the league again. However, undaunted, I played out another series with the same inexorable result—my ultimate defeat. And another series. And another one. . . .

After eight years or so of this, Ben was still questioning. "Don't you get discouraged?" Ben said to me one day with an over-hearty chuckle. "Never," I retorted. "I'm younger than you. You'll get senile sooner or later, and then I'll win for sure. Time is on my side."

Jock

Intimacy

Jock and I had become close friends as we began to work together, sharing our offices and our insights with one another. Recognizing that one of the major issues for the people we were seeing was one of intimacy, we decided to explore as many of the parameters of this subject as we were able to in our developing relationship; it was to be a personal project. The experimental design was simple—we agreed to provide one another with instant access to our inner worlds, ready to reveal what was happening at any given moment. Furthermore, we agreed to acknowledge whatever either of us was doing—fears, judgments, prejudices, etc. that would interfere with intimacy. It all seemed so easy! It was not.

Very quickly, each of us was facing difficult inner truths from which we had shielded ourselves. As with most people, our defenses were strong and too effective. We began to discover why most people would prefer to be in control of one another, invulnerable and irresponsible for the self. But our greatest fear was sexuality. Like the rest of society, we believed that when we became truly intimate, then we would discover our sexual excitement for one another. As a matter of fact, the term "intimacy" was used synonymously and euphemistically with sexual behaviour, as in "Are you being intimate?" to mean "Are you having sexual relations?" Although I had little problem with that possibility, Jock was particularly freaked over the possibility, as so much of his identity has been tied to a macho, sexually attractive, heterosexual image. In spite of that, he stuck to his commitment to explore the depths of intimacy between us.

The closer we got, the more nervous Jock became. In the very beginnings of our relationship, before we began to live together, every time that we would have an emotionally close experience, he would physically disappear from my world for months. His excuses were always along the line that he was too busy or too involved in other things. Now that we were living together, escape seemed impossible. Instead of physically absenting himself, he would become emotionally distant and non-present. My supposition was that he was reacting unconsciously to his fear of discovering some possible sexual excitement with me.

We persisted with our project, feeling closer and closer as we continued to unearth our defenses against intimacy. Finally, we crossed some major barrier while attending a convention in Banff. We each were lying nude in our own single beds in the darkness of our hotel room when I heard Jock's nervous voice hesitatingly break through the darkness. "Ben, should we check out our sexual feelings for one another? I could come over to your bed," Jock said tentatively. "Of course," I replied. "Come on over." Jock quickly crossed the room and climbed under the covers with me.

Our hearts beating wildly in the darkness, we lay side by side like boards, on our backs, our arms stretched down by our sides. After what seemed to be an eternity, Jock spoke into the darkness, "I don't feel anything, Ben. Do you?" At his side, I too spoke into the darkness. "No," I said, and heard him exhale a deep sigh of relief in response. "Then," he said, "I might as well go back to my own bed."

Although this was only the first of many similar experiences, we discovered over and over again that even though we were reaching phenomenal depths of intimacy, it was not accompanied by sexual excitement. After working with thousands of people who were prepared to be honest about their own sexual feelings, we have found that this is an experience common to many others. We have arrived at the conclusion that intimacy and sexual excitement are two separate phenomena that can be linked together, but that are not naturally or instinctively so. As a matter of fact, it even appears that in intimate relationships, the sexual excitement is strongest when the persons know one another the least. Although in the early stages of a relationship the safety of a committed relationship may allow for a freer expression of hitherto repressed sexual impulses, their sexual excitement tends to diminish when people become known to one another intimately.

Now, for both of us, whether we have sexual feelings for one another is of very little consequence. We realize that the only essential element is that we love one another.

Rejection

At first, Ben and I had no romance in our relationship together. We were two dedicated scientists, studying relationships in the laboratory of our friendship. The project was fascinating, but not romantic. As Ben will describe, we came in time to produce our own little romances to spice up our relationship. And we both learned to feel romantic in our cute little expectations of each other. The feeling of being important to someone else was delicious, and we both came to enjoy it thoroughly.

One day, we were travelling together by car from Vancouver to Seattle. Ben was driving and I was the passenger, with time to think and reflect. Feeling a little unsure of myself, I thought, "I wonder if he really loves me? If he does, he should demonstrate some sign of it." Driving along, the fantasy became more clear, and I thought, "If he truly loves me, he'll spontaneously reach out and touch me with an affectionate gesture."

We drove on. I waited expectantly for his spontaneous outpouring of affection. As the miles went by, I became less insecure and more irritated that he was not demonstrating his affection. Gradually, I became hurt, and then quite angry. Just outside Seattle, I said, "Stop the car! I'm getting out! If I don't matter any more than this to you, I don't want to continue travelling together!"

Ben pulled over and looked at me with a puzzled expression. "What do you mean?" he asked. "I have been feeling so fond of you during this whole trip." I said, "But if you really cared, you would have expressed your affection with a little touch." He replied, "I would have been glad to. But I didn't know that it was expected or required. Does my love have to be packaged in a specific way?"

In a flood of embarrassment, I realized that I was mistaking the form for the feeling. I was looking for an outward expression that I had

predetermined meant loving; I was missing that he was feeling loving all the time. I wondered how many other times I have missed
people's feelings because they were not expressing them in the manner that I had predetermined. I am still reflecting on this sobering
thought.

Jock

Jealousy

Early in our relationship, when we believed that sexual excitement would naturally occur with intimacy, Jock and I became sexually celibate, awaiting the
dreaded day of discovering sexual feelings for one another. After several years of
such celibacy, I noticed that without sexual experience, Jock was slipping into a
state of apathy. The dynamic, macho person I had been attracted to was dying,
replaced by a mere shadow of the person I had known. One morning, I expressed this concern to him, wondering if he ought to follow his sexual desire.

In what seemed to me to be unnecessary haste, he agreed and was on the phone
in minutes, arranging a date for that very evening! As he did so, I felt a pang of
concern. With enthusiasm, Jock began to prepare for his date, scrubbing, shav-
ing, and arranging clothing, humming all the while. My anxiety level mounted
as I became incapable of carrying on with my normal day. Seeing him so happy
over the prospect of being with somebody other than myself, I found myself
uttering nonsensical statements that I never knew were stored within myself.
"What's wrong with me?" I would ask Jock, as though his enjoying somebody
else was a negative judgment on who and what I am. There was nothing wrong
with me! I began to realize that for the first time in our relationship, I was
experiencing the pain of jealousy!

Very soon, it occurred to me that my pain was stemming from a childhood fear
of abandonment as I felt unworthy of being valued by others. It was clear that
my jealousy was my attempt to *control* Jock's behaviour so that I would not be
abandoned. And I had believed that I had grown beyond such emotions! I felt

triumphant over discovering this about myself. However, the pain and jealousy only continued to grow. Insight offered no relief. Instead, the hurt only grew stronger as the day progressed.

I found myself beginning to weep uncontrollably as I heard my voice exclaiming, "What has *she* got that I haven't got?" Was I going crazy? I knew the answer to that question; after all, I was a doctor! Nevertheless, these kinds of questions just seemed to roll out of my mouth as I paced the floor and worked myself into a frenzy. I was too miserable and Jock was too excited to eat. So he just continued to prepare and I continued to pace.

As the fateful hour of his departure arrived, I was beside myself with grief and pain as I went to the door to hug him farewell. By this time, he was really concerned about my welfare, not wishing to be the cause of so much grief. Both of us knew that I was the only one responsible for my pain; yet his compassion for me was quickly being converted into guilt. At the door, he said that he couldn't stand to see me suffer so much. "I can't go out on this date!" he proclaimed.

I was furious! I berated him for his cowardice over this matter; I had already paid for this event with so much pain that he could at least tolerate the relatively minor pain of his own guilt. He would have to live up to his end of his bargain whether he wanted to or not! If he were to be controlled over my jealousy, then we would never be able to break through this awful impasse.

As I hugged him and pushed him out the door, I said, "Get out there and enjoy yourself!" Under my breath, I added, "But be careful when you come home not to light a match because my head is going to be in the oven!" Little matter that we had an electric stove.

Since that historical event, Jock has continued to pursue his sexual excitement and I have continued to process my anxiety and jealousy. Later, the tables were turned; now we each have had experience on all sides of that issue. All of this has been important to provide us with what we have needed to grow and mature so that we can truly be intimate with one another. Our project has remained on track.

Avoiding Abandonment

For all my remembered life, I have been afraid of being abandoned. And so, I have been a pleaser, eager to maintain control over others by not providing any reason to be left. Pleasing, grovelling, patronizing, seducing, manipulation of all kinds—these have been my coin to prevent my most feared circumstance, being left. When Ben would withdraw, I would feel a sense of panic and a desperation to coerce him into returning to me as quickly as possible. Hence, I remained field dependent, needing to please in order to keep Ben with me.

And then one day came the miraculous shift. Ben had withdrawn, and fell into a self-protective snooze on the couch. Stunned, I remained next to him, and observed his sleeping form. I felt sad, and dejected, and rejected. I was ready to go into my panic about being left, when curiosity intervened. I noticed that I also felt a warmth and concern for my sleeping friend, who was obviously also hurting. And in my concern for him, I did not retreat into the self-pity and dejection at being abandoned. Ben had withdrawn, and I had stayed with him. I enjoyed the following minutes, feeling warm and compassionate and very present with him. And the thought struck: "Just because he leaves me doesn't mean I have to react by leaving him; I can stay present when he leaves. Indeed, I can stay with him, and even go where he goes."

From that day on, when Ben says, "If that's the way it is, I'm leaving," I find myself saying, "OK, I'll pack a bag. Where are we going?"

Jock

The people in one's life are like the pillars on one's porch you see life through. And sometimes they hold you up, and sometimes they lean on you, and sometimes it is just enough to know they're standing by.

. . . M. Shain[19]

From Romance to Power Struggle

Jock and I had agreed to investigate the meanings of intimacy. As we were succeeding at feeling close with a real knowing of one another, we realized that we didn't have a romantic way of acknowledging that to one another. We were two men without any experience of having role models to copy. It was the early eighties; as yet, society had not offered open expressions of how romance was to be expressed between two persons of the same sex. All that was available were examples of camaraderie of men in the pub or at war at one extreme, and of homosexual sexuality at the other. We realized that we fit none of these categories.

Initially, we turned to mythology, our usual source of inspiration. There, we found very little. Damon and Pythias first came to mind. Pythias had been condemned to death but requested leave to arrange family affairs. Damon agreed to replace him and be executed if he did not return; but return he did at the very last moment. The Syracuse king Dionysus I was so impressed by their friendship that he forgave them. Although that story was becoming appropriate for us, it offered little for us to emulate as a way of celebration.

Other myths that we considered were the ones of David and Jonathan or Achilles and Patroclus, but all of them seemed too remote to us. No, we needed a more contemporary role model. Looking at the heterosexual world, we struck upon television as the chief purveyor of modern myths. Upon examining reruns of *The Donna Reed Show*, we saw that the couple kissed one another as he went off to work and she stayed at home to mind the kids. We could do that because we lived together; the only difference was that we both went off to work. However, we soon established a routine of a goodbye kiss and hug before emerging from our back door.

Over the months, as with any romance, that routine took on major significance. Failure to perform this ritual was a signal of being out of touch with one another, whether due to mindlessness or an unresolved argument. It did not matter how perfunctory the ritual was, it only mattered that it was performed—how like most marriages that we knew!

One day, realizing that our ritual had become routinized, and that I had much more feeling than a quick peck and hug could signify, I decided to be more exuberant, more closely matching how I really felt about Jock. Unfortunately, our back hall was too cramped a space for much exuberance, so in preparation for the event, I stepped outside to wait for him by the back door. All of a sudden, the door flew open with a bang and Jock stormed past me. Before I had a chance to question his behaviour or to explain my own, he muttered some expletives that added up to: "If *that* is how little I mean to you ...." as he raced into the car.

Thus began another power struggle, all over a simple misunderstanding!

Romance is a function of fiction and imagination, encompassing both the possible and impossible. Even when it appears to be filled with light (as with our penchant towards hope), it grows in the dark, fed by ignorance and denial. Romance clouds our consciousness, deludes our rationality and results in faulty decision-making. It undermines our confidence and makes fools of us all.

Yet, a life without romance would hardly be worth living. Whatever we construe to be a meaning in life is a product of our romance-ability!

... Jock McKeen and Bennet Wong

Flow

Whenever we work together, Ben and I enjoy a feeling of flow that comes with being tuned in and sensitive to each other. People often marvel at how responsive we are to each other, one person moving to speak while the other is just completing a thought. Some have described our public presentations as a dance between two very attuned partners. Well, this did not come easily; and it was not always thus.

When we were first working together, we were invited to give a public speech to a large professional group. As a young, inexperienced doctor, I was somewhat overwhelmed by the challenge of speaking in front of so many people. I was nervous; however, I covered my discomfort under a veneer of confidence. Underneath, I was terrified. All the images of being a fat, inadequate kid, harassed by bullies after school, came back. I thought, "No one will want to listen to me. I'll make a fool of myself." Ben said, "Just be yourself, and at the least, it will be a learning experience."

Before our presentation, we discussed the general outline of the talk, and agreed that one person would yield the microphone when the other made a motion towards it, to make for a flowing presentation. I was afraid that I might be struck mute and might not have anything to say to cause me to move toward the microphone at all. Before the lecture, facing the audience, I stared out at a sea of a thousand faces and nervously put on my best professional facial expression. As the lecture began, Ben spoke his introductory remarks, and remarkably, in my mind, something formed for me to say! I edged toward the microphone; sensitively, Ben moved away, and I smoothly moved in to speak. After a short time, I sensed him at my elbow, and yielded to his verbal input. As I calmed down, I permitted thoughts to enter, such as "This is going very well. They like us. There is nothing to be nervous about; public speaking is a breeze!"

I was beginning to get a heady feeling of success. All my early days when I was inept, unassured, and apologetic faded to the back of my mind as I tasted the power of the microphone. I looked out, and everyone seemed to be hanging upon my every word. I tossed them another idea, and the crowd seemed to nod and sway approvingly. I had them in the palm of my hand! I became like the mad scientist. Crazed, wild-eyed with newfound power and fame, I lectured on.

I sensed some pressure on my arm. However, I lingered in front of the microphone to finish up the pearls of wisdom that I was spreading to the worshipping multitudes before me. The pressure became more insistent, and I darted a sidelong glance to see Ben glowering at me (subtly, but definitely with a lot of heat). Although I had many more morsels of my genius to distribute, I reluctantly yielded the microphone to him. The rest of the talk is a blur to me.

Afterwards, sitting in a coffee shop to debrief, I faced the full extent of his anger. "You were just up there to aggrandize your own indulgences! You lost touch with me, and the audience, and your own sensitivity! You abandoned your presence!"

Ashamedly, I admitted that this was so. I had become so caught up in the frenzy of my excitement at being seen as important that I let go of my agreement to work in flow with Ben. And so I had shortchanged him, the audience, and myself.

Sobered and humbled, I recognized the extent of my power craving. The next time we came to give a public talk, I was nervous again, but this time for a different reason. By then I knew that I could speak in front of audiences, and that I had things to say. This time I was nervous that I might give in to my cravings for power and lose touch again. And so, I became vigilant about being sensitive to the audience, to Ben, and to myself.

Over the years, I have struggled with this process. The struggle has been fruitful; for from it has come a genuine flow and responsiveness between the two of us. However, I had not imagined that finding a feeling of flow would have taken so much work and attention!

Jock

The Landscape of Our Lives

I have found that people tend to be goal-directed. They frequently wish to fix some problems in their lives, to let go of unfortunate situations, to forget unhappy relationships, to finally "deal with" their feelings about the past, to be able to face the future changed and unimpeded. After devoting much time and money to counsellors and other people helpers, they are often astonished to discover their demons are still with them. For myself, I now have arrived at the belief that nothing will ever be finished, that we will never be rid of the past, and that ultimately the essentials about ourselves will never change!

I have shifted from a belief that human experience is a linear affair from past to present to future, to a belief that each of our lives is an immutable landscape of experience. We all have our mountains of exhilaration, surrounded by our cliffs of danger and hardships. Each of us has places of contentment and placidity, like soothing lakes and gentle forests; similarly, each has deep, exciting, and sometimes threatening waters as well as scary, unknown jungles. There are in everyone various parched deserts and lush, productive wetlands. Each of our landscapes is endless in its variety of appearances and experiences.

Although the choices are numerous, most people tend to limit themselves to living in only a few parts of the total possibilities. Some people are mountain people while others tend to live in their valleys. However, no matter in which part of their landscape they may find themselves, if they would look carefully in all directions, they would see that the entire landscape is always there—in the *background*. What they are experiencing has only moved into the foreground. Nothing has been exterminated or altered. All that has changed has been the location of the present experience.

So, when experiencing happiness, a person should be aware that somewhere in the background still lurks an area of sadness. While experiencing joy in the foreground, despair has only been relegated to the background at that time. Some people become fixated to one location; even when they are in safe and happy circumstances, they are unable to shift the dangerous, harmful childhood experiences from their foreground into the background. Thus, such a person is anxious and depressed even when the current context would provide ideal circumstances for security and pleasure. By remaining stuck in one area of the landscape, this person has diminished the scope of experience; the landscape has become a small window of the whole larger picture. Such a narrowing and fixation is what accounts for "neurosis."

If this metaphor of life is understood, it would seem that to ensure good mental health, people should be encouraged to visit all parts of their landscape to remain aware of the wide range of possibilities of experience. If they are able to remain flexible enough to shift readily, not forced to remain rigidly in one place (as occurs in a fixed moral position), they will be able to stay attuned to present circumstances. That would be a sign of good mental health.

Such a metaphor begs the consideration of another set of dynamics. What if the person were unable to sustain a portion of the landscape for a reasonable length of time? Such is the case in people who experience sudden shifts and wide ranges of movement. Foreground and background are unable to remain constant. The person experiences severe dislocation, unable to have a stable sense of identification. They are described by outside observers as being "all over the map." The sustainability of foreground is another sign of good mental health.

Now that I have this picture of mental health, I no longer waste energy trying to "fix" anything. I now focus more on helping myself and other people to more easily move through our personal landscapes.

The Pit

When I am working with people, a topic commonly reported to me is a loathing and fear of moving into a part of the personal landscape that is universally referred to as "the pit." At times, such experience is named or described as a "pit or well of despair," the "void," the " blackness," the "chaos," and the "meaninglessness." Apparently, we all have one, although most would prefer to deny it; as we travel through our landscapes, most of us give our "pits" a wide berth.

No matter how much we attempt to avoid the pit, it seems that we always tend to slide toward it and into it. Many of us have found that if we move fast enough, as with centrifugal force, rapidly running around the brink through busy-ness, obsessions and compulsions, we can avoid the inevitable slippage. Of course, by becoming so occupied, we fail to explore all the many other aspects of our landscapes, and our worlds become narrow and rigid. Furthermore, deep and meaningful relationships are impossible to establish and maintain.

Such a picture of life is and has been very unappealing. In the past, all of this movement was justified by a belief in a god (capital "G" God in western cultures). We were admonished to run quickly, work hard, and suffer long, because the more we did so, the greater the reward we would enjoy sometime later. With Judaism and Christianity, the pit was dealt with by the positing of a God that lived in Heaven on the other side of the cliffs of Life. Instead of sliding into the Pit, we were encouraged to scale the mountainside, painful and difficult as that may be, because on the "other side," after death, we were promised an eternal resting place with God in Heaven. There, after suffering Life's trials and tribulations, so long as we remained faithful to God's commandments, we would be rewarded with eternal milk and honey. Such future rewards made suffering acceptable.

Picture us hanging on with desperate fingernails, always looking upward to the top of the mountain, on the other side of which we could spend eternity in Heaven with our God. We began to hear voices from the other side of the mountain calling out to us, "Hey, there's nothing over here—no Heaven, no God!" Hearing those "No God" theories was not good news to all who were suffering. Suddenly, digging in and climbing to the top made no sense at all.

So many stopped climbing. As they did, they began to slip downward; looking below, they got glimpses of the Pit into which they were being drawn. At this time, some gave up and sank into meaninglessness and oblivion; others decided to live it up and party all the time on their way down. The more fortunate decided to expand their horizons, becoming more aware of the backgrounds of their landscape. They decided to explore their inner territories, to experience the length and breadth of their dominions. The more flexible they were, and the more curiosity they possessed, the more interesting and broadening were their journeys. They discovered whole new worlds emerging into the foreground of their consciousness. Their pits receded into the background, even though they did not disappear.

The promise of future rewards is no longer necessary. In the present, life is full!

All neurosis is, at root, an issue of loss of faith.

. . . Bennet Wong

Reps' Stories

Paul Reps, the Zen master, lived the last few years of his life at Haven with us. He was full of wise and pithy sayings, and was always responding in insightful and unexpected ways. He seemed to simply be having fun; but at the same time, in the midst of his antics and sharp quips, there were many lessons to be learned.

"Joined"
Reps would not come to sit at our table at lunch. I talked with him about this, and he said, "You guys have important business to talk about, and I don't want to get in the way." I replied, "Reps, you are always welcome to join us."

"Already joined!" Reps said. "Don't you know that?"

Reincarnation
A participant in a workshop once asked, "Reps, do you believe in reincarnation?" He replied, "Ask me that again."

Again the question, "Reps, do you believe in reincarnation?" He replied, "Ask me that again."

And again, "Reps, do you believe in reincarnation?" He replied, "Ask me that again."

Then, "Reps, do you believe in reincarnation?" He replied, "Ask me that again."

"Reps, do you believe in reincarnation?" He replied, "Ask me that again."

Her incredulous face showed that she didn't get his lesson. She stopped asking verbally; however, she went away puzzled, and wondering—which is just what the old wizard had intended.

How Do You Know?
Very politely, I introduced a friend to Reps, saying, "Reps, this is Josie." His reply: "How do you know?"

Reps Poems
One day, Reps came to me very excitedly, and announced, "I've just written a poem. Do you want to hear it?" Of course I did, and asked him to speak it. He stood up like a polite schoolboy and recited:

"Incredible as it may seem . . . it may seem!"

Another Reps poem:

Where is Jesus? Where is Buddha?
In the dust.
Where is John? Where is Mary?
In the must.

Change in Diet
We asked him about his ravenous appetite, and wondered at his capacity. We said, "We thought that you have lived simply and in Zen tradition all your life. How do you explain all your eating?"

Reps replied, "I realize now that all my life, I've been starving myself. I didn't realize food could be so good!"

He delighted in food. He announced one day over a meal of freshly caught fish that we were eating "a live salmon." And his sweet tooth also gave him away. He once volunteered, "Under the influence of this cake, I will sign anything!"

Death
As he got older, he showed his disregard for the sentimental fixation on ceremony. He once told me, "When I die, just throw the body into a ditch."

Time

One time, Reps became fascinated with a small computer device that would give an oracle in the form of the *I Ching*, the ancient Chinese Book of Changes. He talked about the "I Ching Decision Science Computer" without cease for a whole month. I would hear a small voice behind me, "I just consulted it again, and again I received very scientific information. This machine is a wonder!" And I kept up the conversation with him. Each time he would meet me, he would continue where we had left off, even though the gap in conversation might have been a couple of days. It was as if we were having an unbroken dialogue.

Reps was planning to go on a trip. One day, I heard the small voice behind me saying, "Before I go away, I'm going to give it to you." I replied, "What are you going to give me?" He replied, "The I Ching Decision Science Computer, of course."

I was thrilled and quite touched. "Thank you, Reps; I'm very honoured that you want to give this to me. I know it's special to you."

Gruffly, he retorted, "You were enthusiastic about it. Therefore you deserve to have it."

I replied, somewhat befuddled, "I wish everything I was enthusiastic about came to me."

Amazed and wide-eyed, he shot back, "It does. Everything you are enthusiastic about comes to you. Don't you know that yet?"

I replied, "Some things are taking quite a long time in coming!"

"Ah yes," he said. "Time—that's another thing!"

Jock

 Our memories are old friends that never tire of reminding us to be humble.

. . . Bennet Wong & Jock McKeen

References

1. P. Tillich, *The Courage To Be* (New Haven: Yale University Press, 1952), p. 89.

2. *An Introduction To Zen* (New York: Peter Pauper Press, 1959), p. 36.

3. Tillich, *The Courage To Be*, p. 89.

4. S. Keen, *Fire In The Belly* (New York: Bantam Books, 1991), p. 42.

5. M. Shain, *When Lovers Are Friends* (New York: Bantam Books, 1979), p. 81.

6. J. Krishnamurti, quoted in E.H. Sell, ed., *The Spirit Of Loving* (Boston: Shambhala, 1995), p. 117.

7. J. Bartlett, *Familiar Quotations* (Boston: Little Brown, 1980), p. 774.

8. C. Fadiman, ed. *The Little, Brown Book of Anecdotes* (Boston: Little, Brown, 1985), p. 500.

9. Shain, *When Lovers Are Friends,* p. 65.

10. J. Sheban, *The Wisdom of Gibran* (New York: Bantam Books, 1973), p. 69.

11. Bartlett, *Familiar Quotations,* p. 676.

12. S. Keen, *Inward Bound* (New York: Bantam Books, 1992), p. 157.

13. A. Watts, *Death* (Millbrae, CA: Celestial Arts, 1975), p. 59.

14. F. Herbert, *Dune* (London: New English Library, 1972), p. 220.

15. Fadiman, *The Little, Brown Book of Anecdotes,* p. 500.

16. Keen, *Inward Bound*, p. 133.

17. R. Dreikurs, *Children: The Challenge* (New York: E.P. Dutton, 1987), p. 186.

18. A. Einstein, quoted in J. Daintith, H. Egerton, R. Fergusson, A. Stibbs, & E. Wright, eds., *The Macmillan Dictionary Of Quotations* (New York: Macmillan, 1989), p. 275.

19. Shain, *When Lovers Are Friends,* p. 106.